PORTFOLIO / PENGUIN

START WITH WHY

SIMON SINEK is an optimist who believes in a brighter future for humanity. His talk on TED.com is the third most watched talk of all time. Learn more about his work and how you can inspire those around you at StartWithWhy.com.

START
WITH WHY

HOW GREAT LEADERS
INSPIRE EVERYONE
TO TAKE ACTION

SIMON SINEK

PORTFOLIO / PENGUIN

PORTFOLIO / PENGUIN
Published by the Penguin Group
Penguin Group (USA) Inc., 375 Hudson Street, New York, New York 10014, U.S.A.
Penguin Group (Canada), 90 Eglinton Avenue East, Suite 700, Toronto, Ontario,
Canada M4P 2Y3 (a division of Pearson Penguin Canada Inc.)
Penguin Books Ltd, 80 Strand, London WC2R 0RL, England
Penguin Ireland, 25 St. Stephen's Green, Dublin 2, Ireland (a division of Penguin Books Ltd)
Penguin Books Australia Ltd, 250 Camberwell Road, Camberwell,
Victoria 3124, Australia (a division of Pearson Australia Group Pty Ltd)
Penguin Books India Pvt Ltd, 11 Community Centre, Panchsheel Park, New Delhi – 110 017, India
Penguin Group (NZ), 67 Apollo Drive, Rosedale, Auckland 0632,
New Zealand (a division of Pearson New Zealand Ltd)
Penguin Books (South Africa) (Pty) Ltd, 24 Sturdee Avenue,
Rosebank, Johannesburg 2196, South Africa

Penguin Books Ltd, Registered Offices: 80 Strand, London WC2R 0RL, England

First published in the United States of America by Portfolio, a member of Penguin Group (USA) Inc. 2009
This paperback edition with a new preface and new afterword published 2011

46th Printing

THE LIBRARY OF CONGRESS HAS CATALOGED THE HARDCOVER EDITION AS FOLLOWS:
Sinek, Simon.
Start with why : how great leaders inspire everyone to take action / by Simon Sinek.
p. cm.
Includes bibliographical references and index.
ISBN 978-1-59184-280-4 (hc.)
ISBN 978-1-59184-644-4 (pbk.)
1. Leadership. I. Title.
HD57.7.S549 2009
658.4'092—dc22   2009021862

Printed in the United States of America
Set in Minion
Designed by Victoria Hartman

There are leaders and there are those who lead.
Leaders hold a position of power or influence.
Those who lead inspire us.

Whether individuals or organizations, we follow those
who lead not because we have to, but because we want to.
We follow those who lead not for them, but for ourselves.

This is a book for those who want to inspire others and
for those who want to find someone to inspire them.

For Victoria,
who finds good ideas
and makes them great

CONTENTS

THE POWER OF WHY

When I first discovered this thing called the WHY, it came at a time in my life when I needed it. It wasn't an academic or intellectual pursuit; I had fallen out of love with my work and found myself in a very dark place. There was nothing wrong with the quality of my work or my job, per se; it was the enjoyment I had for that work that I'd lost. By all superficial measurements, I should have been happy. I made a good living. I worked with great clients. The problem was, I didn't feel it. I was no longer fulfilled by my work and I needed to find a way to rekindle my passion.

The discovery of WHY completely changed my view of the world and discovering my own WHY restored my passion to a degree multiple times greater than at any other time in my life. It was such a simple, powerful, and actionable idea, that I shared it with my friends. That's what we do when we find something of value, we share it with the people we love. Inspired, my friends started making big life changes. In turn, they invited me to share this idea with their friends, the people they loved. And so the idea started to spread.

It was at this point I decided to turn myself into the guinea pig. It didn't seem right that I would share or promote a concept that I didn't practice myself. So I was going to practice it as wholly as I could. The only reason I am where I am today, this representative of WHY, is for one reason and one reason only: because of other people.

I have no publicist. I have had only very little national press coverage. Yet the concept of WHY is spreading far and wide because it resonates with people on such a visceral level that they share it with those they love and care about. That I was given the opportunity to write a book about the concept has allowed the depth of the idea to spread without me. The TEDx Talk I gave that was posted on ted.com continues to spread far and wide not because of any social media strategy. It spreads because this message is inherently optimistic. It is inherently human. And those who believe in it share it.

The more organizations and people who learn to also start with WHY, the more people there will be who wake up feeling fulfilled by the work they do. And that's about the best reason I can think of to continue sharing this idea.

Inspire on!

Simon Sinek
New York
July 28, 2011

INTRODUCTION

WHY START WITH WHY?

This book is about a naturally occurring pattern, a way of thinking, acting and communicating that gives some leaders the ability to inspire those around them. Although these "natural-born leaders" may have come into the world with a predisposition to inspire, the ability is not reserved for them exclusively. We can all learn this pattern. With a little discipline, any leader or organization can inspire others, both inside and outside their organization, to help advance their ideas and their vision. We can all learn to lead.

The goal of this book is not simply to try to fix the things that aren't working. Rather, I wrote this book as a guide to focus on and amplify the things that do work. I do not aim to upset the solutions offered by others. Most of the answers we get, when based on sound evidence, are perfectly valid. However, if we're starting with the wrong questions, if we don't understand the cause, then even the right answers will always steer us wrong . . . eventually. The truth, you see, is always revealed . . . eventually.

The stories that follow are of those individuals and organizations that naturally embody this pattern. They are the ones that start with Why.

I.

The goal was ambitious. Public interest was high. Experts were eager to contribute. Money was readily available.

Armed with every ingredient for success, Samuel Pierpont Langley set out in the early 1900s to be the first man to pilot an airplane. Highly regarded, he was a senior officer at the Smithsonian Institution, a mathematics professor who had also worked at Harvard. His friends included some of the most powerful men in government and business, including Andrew Carnegie and Alexander Graham Bell. Langley was given a $50,000 grant from the War Department to fund his project, a tremendous amount of money for the time. He pulled together the best minds of the day, a veritable dream team of talent and know-how. Langley and his team used the finest materials, and the press followed him everywhere. People all over the country were riveted to the story, waiting to read that he had achieved his goal. With the team he had gathered and ample resources, his success was guaranteed.

Or was it?

A few hundred miles away, Wilbur and Orville Wright were working on their own flying machine. Their passion to fly was so intense that it inspired the enthusiasm and commitment of a dedicated group in their hometown of Dayton, Ohio. There was no funding for their venture. No government grants. No high-level connections. Not a single person on the team had an advanced degree or even a college education, not even Wilbur or Orville. But the team banded together in a humble bicycle shop and made their vision real. On December 17, 1903, a small group witnessed a man take flight for the first time in history.

How did the Wright brothers succeed where a better-equipped, better-funded and better-educated team could not?

It wasn't luck. Both the Wright brothers and Langley were highly motivated. Both had a strong work ethic. Both had keen scientific minds. They were pursuing exactly the same goal, but only the Wright brothers were able to inspire those around them and truly lead their team to develop a technology that would change the world. Only the Wright brothers started with Why.

2.

In 1965, students on the campus of the University of California, Berkeley, were the first to publicly burn their draft cards to protest America's involvement in the Vietnam War. Northern California was a hotbed of antigovernment and antiestablishment sentiment; footage of clashes and riots in Berkeley and Oakland was beamed around the globe, fueling sympathetic movements across the United States and Europe. But it wasn't until 1976, nearly three years after the end of America's military involvement in the Vietnam conflict, that a different revolution ignited.

They aimed to make an impact, a very big impact, even challenge the way people perceived how the world worked. But these young revolutionaries did not throw stones or take up arms against an authoritarian regime. Instead, they decided to beat the system at its own game. For Steve Wozniak and Steve Jobs, the cofounders of Apple Computer, the battlefield was business and the weapon of choice was the personal computer.

The personal computer revolution was beginning to brew when Wozniak built the Apple I. Just starting to gain attention, the technology was primarily seen as a tool for business. Computers were too complicated and out of the price range of the average individual. But Wozniak, a man not motivated by money, envisioned a nobler purpose for the technology. He saw the personal computer as a way for the little man to take on a corporation. If he could figure out a way to get it in the hands of the individual, he thought, the computer would give nearly anyone the ability to perform many of the same functions as a vastly better resourced company. The personal computer could level the playing field and change the way the world operated. Woz designed the Apple I, and improved the technology with the Apple II, to be affordable and simple to use.

No matter how visionary or how brilliant, a great idea or a great product isn't worth much if no one buys it. Wozniak's best friend at the time, the twenty-one-year-old Steve Jobs, knew exactly what to do. Though he had experience selling surplus electronics parts, Jobs would prove to be much more than a good salesman. He wanted to do something significant in the world, and building a company was how he was going to do it. Apple was the tool he used to ignite his revolution.

In their first year in business, with only one product, Apple made a million dollars in revenues. By year two, they did $10 million in sales. In their fourth year, they sold $100 million worth of computers. And in just six years, Apple Computer was a billion-dollar company with over 3,000 employees.

Jobs and Woz were not the only people taking part in the personal computer revolution. They weren't the only smart guys in the business; in fact, they didn't know much about business at all. What made Apple special was not their ability to build such a fast-growth company. It wasn't their ability to think differently about personal computers. What has made Apple special is that they've been able to repeat the pattern over and over and over. Unlike any of their competitors, Apple has successfully challenged conventional thinking within the computer industry, the small electronics industry, the music industry, the mobile phone industry and the broader entertainment industry. And the reason is simple. Apple inspires. Apple starts with Why.

3.

He was not perfect. He had his complexities. He was not the only one who suffered in a pre–civil rights America, and there were plenty of other charismatic speakers. But Martin Luther King Jr. had a gift. He knew how to inspire people.

Dr. King knew that if the civil rights movement was to succeed, if there was to be a real, lasting change, it would take more than him and his closest allies. It would take more than rousing words and eloquent speeches. It would take people, tens of thousands of average citizens, united by a single vision, to change the country. At 11:00 a.m. on August 28, 1963, they would send a message to Washington that it was time for America to steer a new course.

The organizers of the civil rights movement did not send out thousands of invitations, nor was there a Web site to check the date. But the people came. And they kept coming and coming. All told, a quarter of a million people descended on the nation's capital in time to hear the words immortalized by history, delivered by the man who would lead a movement that would change America forever: "I have a dream."

The ability to attract so many people from across the country, of all colors and races, to join together on the right day, at the right time, took something special. Though others knew what had to change in America to bring about civil rights for all, it was Martin Luther King who was able to inspire a country to change not just for the good of a minority, but for the good of everyone. Martin Luther King started with Why.

. . .

There are leaders and there are those who lead. With only 6 percent market share in the United States and about 3 percent worldwide, Apple is not a leading manufacturer of home computers. Yet the company leads the computer industry and is now a leader in other industries as well. Martin Luther King's experiences were not unique, yet he inspired a nation to change. The Wright brothers were not the strongest contenders in the race to take the first manned, powered flight, but they led us into a new era of aviation and, in doing so, completely changed the world we live in.

Their goals were not different than anyone else's, and their systems and processes were easily replicated. Yet the Wright brothers, Apple and Martin Luther King stand out among their peers. They stand apart from the norm and their impact is not easily copied. They are members of a very select group of leaders who do something very, very special. They inspire us.

Just about every person or organization needs to motivate

others to act for some reason or another. Some want to motivate a purchase decision. Others are looking for support or a vote. Still others are keen to motivate the people around them to work harder or smarter or just follow the rules. The ability to motivate people is not, in itself, difficult. It is usually tied to some external factor. Tempting incentives or the threat of punishment will often elicit the behavior we desire. General Motors, for example, so successfully motivated people to buy their products that they sold more cars than any other automaker in the world for over seventy-seven years. Though they were leaders in their industry, they did not lead.

Great leaders, in contrast, are able to inspire people to act. Those who are able to inspire give people a sense of purpose or belonging that has little to do with any external incentive or benefit to be gained. Those who truly lead are able to create a following of people who act not because they were swayed, but because they were inspired. For those who are inspired, the motivation to act is deeply personal. They are less likely to be swayed by incentives. Those who are inspired are willing to pay a premium or endure inconvenience, even personal suffering. Those who are able to inspire will create a following of people—supporters, voters, customers, workers—who act for the good of the whole not because they have to, but because they want to.

Though relatively few in number, the organizations and leaders with the natural ability to inspire us come in all shapes and sizes. They can be found in both the public and private sectors. They are in all sorts of industries—selling to consumers or to other businesses. Regardless of where they exist, they all have a disproportionate amount of influence in their industries. They have the most loyal customers and the most loyal employees. They tend to be more profitable than others in their industry. They are more innovative, and most importantly, they are able to sustain all these things over the long term. Many of them change industries. Some of them even change the world.

The Wright brothers, Apple and Dr. King are just three examples. Harley-Davidson, Disney and Southwest Airlines are three more. John F. Kennedy and Ronald Reagan were also able to inspire. No matter from where they hail, they all have something in common. All the inspiring leaders and companies, regardless of size or industry, think, act and communicate exactly alike.

And it's the complete opposite of everyone else.

What if we could all learn to think, act and communicate like those who inspire? I imagine a world in which the ability to inspire is practiced not just by a chosen few, but by the majority. Studies show that over 80 percent of Americans do not have their dream job. If more knew how to build organizations that inspire, we could live in a world in which that statistic was the reverse—a world in which over 80 percent of people loved their jobs. People who love going to work are more productive and more creative. They go home happier and have happier families. They treat their colleagues and clients and customers better. Inspired employees make for stronger companies and stronger economies. That is why I wrote this book. I hope to inspire others to do the things that inspire them so that together we may build the companies, the economy and a world in which trust and loyalty are the norm and not the exception. This book is not designed to tell you what to do or how to do it. Its goal is not to give you a course of action. Its goal is to offer you the *cause* of action.

For those who have an open mind for new ideas, who seek to create long-lasting success and who believe that your success requires the aid of others, I offer you a challenge. From now on, start with Why.

PART I

A WORLD THAT DOESN'T START WITH WHY

1

ASSUME YOU KNOW

On a cold January day, a forty-three-year-old man was sworn in as the chief executive of his country. By his side stood his predecessor, a famous general who, fifteen years earlier, had commanded his nation's armed forces in a war that resulted in the defeat of Germany. The young leader was raised in the Roman Catholic faith. He spent the next five hours watching parades in his honor and stayed up celebrating until three o'clock in the morning.

You know who I'm describing, right?

It's January 30, 1933, and I'm describing Adolf Hitler and not, as most people would assume, John F. Kennedy.

The point is, we make assumptions. We make assumptions about the world around us based on sometimes incomplete or false information. In this case, the information I offered was incomplete. Many of you were convinced that I was describing John F. Kennedy until I added one minor little detail: the date.

This is important because our behavior is affected by our assumptions or our perceived truths. We make decisions based on what we *think* we know. It wasn't too long ago that the majority of people believed the world was flat. This perceived truth impacted behavior. During this period, there was very little exploration. People feared that if they traveled too far they might fall off the edge of the earth. So for the most part they stayed put. It wasn't until that minor detail was revealed—the world is round—that behaviors changed on a massive scale. Upon this discovery, societies began to traverse the planet. Trade routes were established; spices were traded. New ideas, like mathematics, were shared between societies which unleashed all kinds of innovations and advancements. The correction of a simple false assumption moved the human race forward.

Now consider how organizations are formed and how decisions are made. Do we really know why some organizations succeed and why others don't, or do we just assume? No matter your definition of success—hitting a target stock price, making a certain amount of money, meeting a revenue or profit goal, getting a big promotion, starting your own company, feeding the poor, winning public office—how we go about achieving our goals is very similar. Some of us just wing it, but most of us try to at least gather some data so we can make educated decisions. Sometimes this gathering process is formal—like conducting polls or market research. And sometimes it's informal, like asking our friends and colleagues for advice or looking back on our own personal experience to provide some perspective. Regardless of the process or the goals, we all want to make educated decisions. More importantly, we all want to make the *right* decisions.

As we all know, however, not all decisions work out to be the right ones, regardless of the amount of data we collect. Sometimes the impact of those wrong decisions is minor, and sometimes it can be catastrophic. Whatever the result, we make decisions based on a perception of the world that may not, in fact, be completely accurate. Just as so many were certain that I was describing John F. Kennedy at the beginning of this section. You were certain you were right. You might even have bet money on it—a behavior based on an assumption. Certain, that is, until I offered that little detail of the date.

Not only bad decisions are made on false assumptions. Sometimes when things go right, we think we know why, but do we really? That the result went the way you wanted does not mean you can repeat it over and over. I have a friend who invests some of his own money. Whenever he does well, it's because of his brains and ability to pick the right stocks, at least according to him. But when he loses money, he always blames the market. I have no issue with either line of logic, but either his success and failure hinge upon his own prescience and blindness or they hinge upon good and bad luck. But it can't be both.

So how can we ensure that all our decisions will yield the best results for reasons that are fully within our control? Logic dictates that more information and data are key. And that's exactly what we do. We read books, attend conferences, listen to podcasts and ask friends and colleagues—all with the purpose of finding out more so we can figure out what to do or how to act. The problem is, we've all been in situations in which we have all the data and get lots of good advice but things still don't go quite right. Or maybe the impact lasted for only a short time, or something happened that we could not foresee. A quick note to all of you who correctly guessed Adolf Hitler at the beginning of the section: the details I gave are the same for both Hitler and John F. Kennedy, it could have been either. You have to be careful what you think you know. Assumptions, you see, even when based on sound research, can lead us astray.

Intuitively we understand this. We understand that even with mountains of data and good advice, if things don't go as expected, it's probably because we missed one, sometimes small but vital detail. In these cases, we go back to all our sources, maybe seek out some new ones, and try to figure out what to do, and the whole process begins again. More data, however, doesn't always help, especially if a flawed assumption set the whole process in motion in the first place. There are other factors that must be considered, factors that exist outside of our rational, analytical, information-hungry brains.

There are times in which we had no data or we chose to ignore the advice or information at hand and just went with our gut and things worked out just fine, sometimes even better than expected. This dance between gut and rational decision-making pretty much covers how we conduct business and even live our lives. We can continue to slice and dice all the options in every direction, but at the end of all the good advice and all the compelling evidence, we're left where we started: how to explain or decide a course of action that yields a desired effect that is repeatable. How can we have 20/20 foresight?

There is a wonderful story of a group of American car executives who went to Japan to see a Japanese assembly line. At the end of the line, the doors were put on the hinges, the same as in America. But something was missing. In the United States, a line worker would take a rubber mallet and tap the edges of the door to ensure that it fit perfectly. In Japan, that job didn't seem to exist. Confused, the American auto executives asked at what point they made sure the door fit perfectly. Their Japanese guide looked at them and smiled sheepishly. "We make sure it fits when we design it." In the Japanese auto plant, they didn't examine the problem and accumulate data to figure out the best solution—they engineered the outcome they wanted from the beginning. If they didn't achieve their desired outcome, they understood it was because of a decision they made at the start of the process.

At the end of the day, the doors on the American-made and Japanese-made cars appeared to fit when each rolled off the assembly line. Except the Japanese didn't need to employ someone to hammer doors, nor did they need to buy any mallets. More importantly, the Japanese doors are likely to last longer and maybe even be more structurally sound in an accident. All this for no other reason than they ensured the pieces fit from the start.

What the American automakers did with their rubber mallets is a metaphor for how so many people and organizations lead. When faced with a result that doesn't go according to plan, a series of perfectly effective short-term tactics are used until the desired outcome is achieved. But how structurally sound are those solutions? So many organizations function in a world of tangible goals and the mallets to achieve them. The ones that achieve more, the ones that get more out of fewer people and fewer resources, the ones with an outsized amount of influence, however, build products and companies and even recruit people that all fit based on the original intention. Even though the outcome may look the same, great leaders understand the value in the things we cannot see.

Every instruction we give, every course of action we set, every result we desire, starts with the same thing: a decision. There are those who decide to manipulate the door to fit to achieve the desired result and there are those who start from somewhere very different. Though both courses of action may yield similar short-term results, it is what we can't see that makes long-term success more predictable for only one. The one that understood why the doors need to fit by design and not by default.

2

CARROTS AND STICKS

Manipulation vs. Inspiration

There's barely a product or service on the market today that customers can't buy from someone else for about the same price, about the same quality, about the same level of service and about the same features. If you truly have a first-mover's advantage, it's probably lost in a matter of months. If you offer something truly novel, someone else will soon come up with something similar and maybe even better.

But if you ask most businesses why their customers are their customers, most will tell you it's because of superior quality, features, price or service. In other words, most companies have no clue why their customers are their customers. This is a fascinating realization. If companies don't know why their customers are their customers, odds are good that they don't know why their employees are their employees either.

If most companies don't really know why their customers are their customers or why their employees are their employees, then how do they know how to attract more employees and encourage loyalty among those they already have? The reality is, most businesses today are making decisions based on a set of incomplete or, worse, completely flawed assumptions about what's driving their business.

There are only two ways to influence human behavior: you can manipulate it or you can inspire it. When I mention manipulation, this is not necessarily pejorative; it's a very common and fairly benign tactic. In fact, many of us have been doing it since we were young. "I'll be your best friend" is the highly effective negotiating tactic employed by generations of children to obtain something they want from a peer. And as any child who has ever handed over candy hoping for a new best friend will tell you, it works.

From business to politics, manipulations run rampant in all forms of sales and marketing. Typical manipulations include: dropping the price; running a promotion; using fear, peer pressure or aspirational messages; and promising innovation to influence behavior—be it a purchase, a vote or support. When companies or organizations do not have a clear sense of why their customers are their customers, they tend to rely on a disproportionate number of manipulations to get what they need. And for good reason. Manipulations work.

Price

Many companies are reluctant to play the price game, but they do so because they know it is effective. So effective, in fact, that the temptation can sometimes be overwhelming. There are few professional services firms that, when faced with an opportunity to land a big piece of business, haven't just dropped their price to make the deal happen. No matter how they rationalized it to themselves or their clients, price is a highly effective manipulation. Drop your prices low enough and people will buy from you. We see it at the end of a retail season when products are "priced to move." Drop the price low enough and the shelves will very quickly clear to make room for the next season's products.

Playing the price game, however, can come at tremendous cost and can create a significant dilemma for the company. For the seller, selling based on price is like heroin. The short-term gain is fantastic, but the more you do it, the harder it becomes to kick the habit. Once buyers get used to paying a lower-than-average price for a product or service, it is very hard to get them to pay more. And the sellers, facing overwhelming pressure to push prices lower and lower in order to compete, find their margins cut slimmer and slimmer. This only drives a need to sell more to compensate. And the quickest way to do that is price again. And so the downward spiral of price addiction sets in. In the drug world, these addicts are called junkies. In the business world, we call them commodities. Insurance. Home computers. Mobile phone service. Any number of packaged goods. The list of commodities created by the price game goes on and on. In nearly every circumstance, the companies that are forced to treat their products as commodities brought it upon themselves. I cannot debate that dropping the price is not a perfectly legitimate way of driving business; the challenge is staying profitable.

Wal-Mart seems to be an exception to the rule. They have built a phenomenally successful business playing the price game. But it also came at a high cost. Scale helped Wal-Mart avoid the inherent weaknesses of a price strategy, but the company's obsession with price above all else has left it scandal-ridden and hurt its reputation. And every one of the company's scandals was born from its attempts to keep costs down so it could afford to offer such low prices.

Price always costs something. The question is, how much are you willing to pay for the money you make?

Promotions

General Motors had a bold goal. To lead the American automotive industry in market share. In the 1950s there were four choices of car manufacturer in the United States: GM, Ford, Chrysler and AMC. Before foreign automakers entered the field, GM dominated. New competition, as one would expect, made that goal harder to maintain. I don't need to provide any data to explain how much has changed in the auto industry in fifty years. But General Motors held fast through most of the last century and maintained its prized dominance.

Since 1990, however, Toyota's share of the U.S. market has more than doubled. By 2007, Toyota's share had climbed to 16.3 percent, from only 7.8 percent. During the same period, GM saw its U.S. market share drop dramatically from 35 percent in 1990 to 23.8 percent in 2007. And in early 2008, the unthinkable happened: U.S. consumers bought more foreign-made automobiles than ones made in America.

Since the 1990s, faced with this onslaught of competition from Japan, GM and the other U.S. automakers have scrambled to offer incentives aimed at helping them hold on to their dwindling share. Heavily promoted with advertising, GM, for one, has offered cash-back incentives of between $500 and $7,000 to customers who bought their cars and trucks. For a long time the promotions worked brilliantly. GM's sales were on the rise again.

But in the long term the incentives only helped to dramatically erode GM's profit margins and put them in a deep hole. In 2007, GM lost $729 per vehicle, in large part due to incentives. Realizing that the model was unsustainable, GM announced it would reduce the amount of the cash-back incentives it offered, and with that reduction, sales plummeted. No cash, no customers. The auto industry had effectively created cash-back junkies out of customers, building an expectation that there's no such thing as full price.

Whether it is "two for one" or "free toy inside," promotions are such common manipulations that we often forget that we're being manipulated in the first place. Next time you're in the market for a digital camera, for example, pay attention to how you make your decision. You'll easily find two or three cameras with the specifications you need—size, number of megapixels, comparable price, good brand name. But perhaps one has a promotion—a free carrying case or free memory card. Given the relative parity of the features and benefits, that little something extra is sometimes all it takes to tip the scale. In the business-to-business world, promotions are called "value added." But the principles are the same—give something away for free to reduce the risk so that someone will do business with you. And like price, promotions work.

The manipulative nature of promotions is so well established in retail that the industry even named one of the principles. They call it breakage. Breakage measures the percentage of customers who fail to take advantage of a promotion and end up paying full price for a product instead. This typically happens when buyers don't bother performing the necessary steps to claim their rebates, a process purposely kept complicated or inconvenient to increase the likelihood of mistakes or inaction to keep that breakage number up.

Rebates typically require the customer to send in a copy of a receipt, cut out a bar code from the packaging and painstakingly fill out a rebate form with details about the product and how it was purchased. Sending in the wrong part of the box or leaving out a detail on the application can delay the rebate for weeks, months, or void it altogether. The rebate industry also has a name for the number of customers who just don't bother to apply for the rebate, or who never cash the rebate check they receive. That's called slippage.

For businesses, the short-term benefits of rebates and other manipulations are clear: a rebate lures customers to pay full price for a product that they may have considered buying only because of the prospect of a partial refund. But nearly 40 percent of those customers never get the lower price they thought they were paying. Call it a tax on the disorganized, but retailers rely on it.

Regulators have stepped up their scrutiny of the rebate industry, but with only limited success. The rebate process remains cumbersome and that means free money for the seller. Manipulation at its best. But at what cost?

Fear

If someone were to hold up a bank with a banana in his pocket, he would be charged with armed robbery. Clearly, no victim was in any danger of being shot, but it is the belief that the robber has a real gun that is considered by the law. And for good reason. Knowing full well that fear will motivate them to comply with his demands, the robber took steps to make his victims afraid. Fear, real or perceived, is arguably the most powerful manipulation of the lot.

"No one ever got fired for hiring IBM," goes the old adage, describing a behavior completely borne out of fear. An employee in a procurement department, tasked with finding the best suppliers for a company, turns down a better product at a better price simply because it is from a smaller company or lesser-known brand. Fear, real or perceived, that his job would be on the line if something went wrong was enough to make him ignore the express purpose of his job, even do something that was not in the company's best interest.

When fear is employed, facts are incidental. Deeply seated in our biological drive to survive, that emotion cannot be quickly wiped away with facts and figures. This is how terrorism works. It's not the statistical probability that one could get hurt by a terrorist, but it's the fear that it might happen that cripples a population.

A powerful manipulator, fear is often used with far less nefarious motivations. We use fear to raise our kids. We use fear to motivate people to obey a code of ethics. Fear is regularly used in public service ads, say to promote child safety or AIDS awareness, or the need to wear seat belts. Anyone who was watching television in the 1980s got a heavy dose of antidrug advertising, including one often-mimicked public service ad from a federal program to combat drug abuse among teenagers: "This is your brain," the man's voice said as he held up a pristine white egg. Then he cracked the egg into a frying pan of spattering hot oil. "This is your brain on drugs. . . . Any questions?"

And another ad intended to scare the hell out of any brash teenager: "Cocaine doesn't make you sexy . . . it makes you dead."

Likewise, when politicians say that their opponent will raise taxes or cut spending on law enforcement, or the evening news alerts you that your health or security are at risk unless you tune in at eleven, both are attempting to seed fear among voters and view-ers, respectively. Businesses also use fear to agitate the insecurity we all have in order to sell products. The idea is that if you don't buy the product or service, something bad could happen to you.

"Every thirty-six seconds, someone dies of a heart attack," states an ad for a local cardiac specialist. "Do you have radon? Your neigh-bor does!" reads the ad on the side of a truck for some company selling a home-pollution-inspection service. And, of course, the insurance industry would like to sell you term life insurance "be-fore it's too late."

If anyone has ever sold you anything with a warning to fear the consequences if you don't buy it, they are using a proverbial gun to your head to help you see the "value" of choosing them over their competitor. Or perhaps it's just a banana. But it works.

Aspirations

"Quitting smoking is the easiest thing I've ever done," said Mark Twain. "I've done it hundreds of times."

If fear motivates us to move away from something horrible, as-pirational messages tempt us toward something desirable. Market-ers often talk about the importance of being aspirational, offering someone something they desire to achieve and the ability to get there more easily with a particular product or service. "Six steps to a happier life." "Work those abs to your dream dress size!" "In six short weeks you can be rich." All these messages manipulate. They tempt us with the things we want to have or to be the person we wish we were.

Though positive in nature, aspirational messages are most ef-fective with those who lack discipline or have a nagging fear or insecurity that they don't have the ability to achieve their dreams on their own (which, at various times for various reasons, is every-one). I always joke that you can get someone to buy a gym mem-bership with an aspirational message, but to get them to go three days a week requires a bit of inspiration. Someone who lives a healthy lifestyle and is in a habit of exercising does not respond to "six easy steps to losing weight." It's those who don't have the lifestyle that are most susceptible. It's not news that a lot of people try diet after diet after diet in an attempt to get the body of their dreams. And no matter the regime they choose, each comes with the qualification that regular exercise and a balanced diet will help boost results. In other words, discipline. Gym memberships tend to rise about 12 percent every January, as people try to fulfill their New Year's aspiration to live a healthier life. Yet only a fraction of those aspiring fitness buffs are still attending the gym by the end of the year. Aspirational messages can spur behavior, but for most, it won't last.

Aspirational messages are not only effective in the consumer market, they also work quite well in business-to-business transactions. Managers of companies, big and small, all want to do well, so they make decisions, hire consultants and implement systems to help them achieve that desired outcome. But all too often, it is not the systems that fail but the ability to maintain them. I can speak from personal experience here. I've implemented a lot of systems or practices over the years to help me "achieve the success to which I aspire," only to find myself back to my old habits two weeks later. I aspire for a system that will help me avoid implementing systems to meet all my aspirations. But I probably wouldn't be able to follow it for very long.

This short-term response to long-term desires is alive and well in the corporate world also. A management consultant friend of mine was hired by a billion-dollar company to help it fulfill its goals and aspirations. The problem was, she explained, no matter the issue, the company's managers were always drawn to the quicker, cheaper option over the better long-term solution. Just like the habitual dieter, "they never have the time or money to do it right the first time," she said of her client, "but they always have the time and money to do it again."

Peer Pressure

"Four out of five dentists prefer Trident," touts the chewing gum advertisement in an attempt to get you to try their product. "A double-blind study conducted at a top university concluded . . ." pushes a late-night infomercial. "If the product is good enough for professionals, it's good enough for you," the advertising eggs on. "With over a million satisfied customers and counting," teases another ad. These are all forms of peer pressure. When marketers report that a majority of a population or a group of experts prefers their product over another, they are attempting to sway the buyer to believing that whatever they are selling is better. The peer pressure works because we believe that the majority or the experts might know more than we do. Peer pressure works not because the majority or the experts are always right, but because we fear that we may be wrong.

Celebrity endorsements are sometimes used to add peer pressure to the sales pitch. "If he uses it," we're supposed to think, "it must be good." This makes sense when we hear Tiger Woods endorse Nike golf products or Titleist golf balls. (Woods's deal with Nike is actually credited for putting the company on the map in the golf world.) But Tiger has also endorsed General Motors cars, management consulting services, credit cards, food and a Tag Heuer watch designed "especially for the golfer." The watch, incidentally, can withstand a 5,000-g shock, a level of shock more likely experienced by the golf ball than the golfer. But Tiger endorsed it, so it must be good. Celebrity endorsements are also used to appeal to our aspirations and our desires to be like them. The most explicit example was Gatorade's "I wanna be like Mike" campaign, which tempted youngsters to grow up and be just like Michael Jordan if they drink Gatorade. With many other examples of celebrity endorsements, however, it is harder to see the connection. Sam Waterston of *Law & Order* fame, for example, sells online trading from TD Ameritrade. But for his celebrity, it's uncertain what an actor famed for convicting homicidal maniacs does for the brand. I guess he's "trustworthy."

Impressionable youth are not the only ones subject to peer pressure. Most of us have probably had an experience of being pressured by a salesman. Have you ever had a sales rep try to sell you some "office solution" by telling you that 70 percent of your competitors are using their service, so why aren't you? But what if 70 percent of your competitors are idiots? Or what if that 70 percent were given so much value added or offered such a low price that they couldn't resist the opportunity? The practice is designed to do one thing and one thing only—to pressure you to buy. To make you feel you might be missing out on something or that everyone else knows but you. Better to go with the majority, right?

To quote my mother, "If your friends put their head in the oven, would you do that too?" Sadly, if Michael Jordan or Tiger Woods was paid to do just that, it might actually start a trend.

Novelty (a.k.a. Innovation)

"In a major innovation in design and engineering, [Motorola] has created a phone of firsts," read a 2004 press release that announced the launch of the mobile phone manufacturer's newest entry to the ultracompetitive mobile phone market. "The combination of metals, such as aircraft-grade aluminum, with new advances, such as an internal antenna and a chemically-etched keypad, led to the formation of a device that measures just 13.9mm thin."

And it worked. Millions of people rushed to get one. Celebrities flashed their RAZRs on the red carpet. Even a prime minister or two was seen talking on one. Having sold over 50 million units, few could argue that the RAZR wasn't a huge success. "By surpassing current mobile expectations, the RAZR represents Motorola's history of delivering revolutionary innovations," said former Motorola CEO Ed Zander of his new wunder-product, "while setting a new bar for future products coming out of the wireless industry."

This one product was a huge financial success for Motorola. This was truly an innovation of monumental proportions.

Or was it?

Less than four years later, Zander was forced out. The stock traded at 50 percent of its average value since the launch of the RAZR, and Motorola's competitors had easily surpassed the RAZR's features and functionalities with equally innovative new phones. Motorola was once again rendered just another mobile phone manufacturer fighting for its piece of the pie. Like so many before it, the company confused innovation with novelty.

Real innovation changes the course of industries or even society. The light bulb, the microwave oven, the fax machine, iTunes. These are true innovations that changed how we conduct business, altered how we live our lives, and, in the case of iTunes, challenged an industry to completely reevaluate its business model. Adding a camera to a mobile phone, for example, is not an innovation— a great feature, for sure, but not industry-altering. With this revised definition in mind, even Motorola's own description of its new product becomes just a list of a few great features: a metal case, hidden antenna, flat keypad and a thin phone. Hardly "revolutionary innovation." Motorola had successfully designed the latest shiny object for people to get excited about . . . at least until a new shiny object came out. And that's the reason these features are more a novelty than an innovation. They are added in an attempt to differentiate, but not reinvent. It's not a bad thing, but it can't be counted on to add any long-term value. Novelty can drive sales— the RAZR proved it—but the impact does not last. If a company adds too many novel ideas too often, it can have a similar impact on the product or category as the price game. In an attempt to differentiate with more features, the products start to look and feel more like commodities. And, like price, the need to add yet another product to the line to compensate for the commoditization ends in a downward spiral.

In the 1970s, there were only two types of Colgate toothpaste. But as competition increased, Colgate's sales started to slip. So the company introduced a new product that included a new feature, the addition of fluoride, perhaps. Then another. Then another. Whitening. Tartar control. Sparkles. Stripes. Each innovation certainly helped boost sales, for a while at least. And so the cycle continued. Guess how many different types of toothpaste Colgate has for you to choose from today? Thirty-two. Today there are thirty-two different types of Colgate toothpaste (excluding the four they make for kids). And given how each company responds to the "innovations" of the other, that means that Colgate's competitors also sell a similar number of variants that offer about the same quality, about the same benefits, at about the same price. There are literally dozens and dozens of toothpastes to choose from, yet there is no data to show that Americans are brushing their teeth more now than they were in the 1970s. Thanks to all this "innovation," it has become almost impossible to know which toothpaste is right for you. So much so that even Colgate offers a link on their Web site called "Need Help Deciding?" If Colgate needs to help us pick one of their products because there are too many variations, how are we supposed to decide when we go to the supermarket without their Web site to help us?

Once again, this is an example of the newest set of shiny objects designed to encourage a trial or a purchase. What companies cleverly disguise as "innovation" is in fact novelty. And it's not only packaged goods that rely on novelty to lure customers; it's a common practice in other industries, too. It works, but rarely if ever does the strategy cement any loyal relationships.

Apple's iPhone has since replaced the Motorola RAZR as the popular must-have new mobile phone. Removing all the buttons and putting a touch screen is not what makes the iPhone innovative, however. Those are brilliant new features. But others can copy those things and it wouldn't redefine the category. There is something else that Apple did that is vastly more significant.

Apple is not only leading how mobile phones are designed, but, in typical Apple fashion, also how the industry functions. In the mobile phone industry, it is the service provider, not the phone manufacturer, that determines all the features and benefits the phone can offer. T-Mobile, Verizon Wireless, Sprint, AT&T all dictate to Motorola, Nokia, Ericsson, LG and others what the phones will do. Then Apple showed up. They announced that they would tell the service provider what the phone would do, not the other way around. AT&T was the only one that agreed, thus earning the company the exclusive deal to offer the new technology. That's the kind of shift that will impact the industry for many years and will extend far beyond a few years of stock boost for the shiny new product.

Novel, huh?

The Price You Pay for the Money You Make

I cannot dispute that manipulations work. Every one of them can indeed help influence behavior and every one of them can help a company become quite successful. But there are trade-offs. Not a single one of them breeds loyalty. Over the course of time, they cost more and more. The gains are only short-term. And they increase the level of stress for both the buyer and the seller. If you have exceptionally deep pockets or are looking to achieve only a short-term gain with no consideration for the long term, then these strategies and tactics are perfect.

Beyond the business world, manipulations are the norm in politics today as well. Just as manipulations can drive a sale but not create loyalty, so too can they help a candidate get elected, but they don't create a foundation for leadership. Leadership requires people to stick with you through thick and thin. Leadership is the ability to rally people not for a single event, but for years. In business, leadership means that customers will continue to support your company even when you slip up. If manipulation is the only strategy, what happens the next time a purchase decision is required? What happens after the election is won?

There is a big difference between repeat business and loyalty. Repeat business is when people do business with you multiple times. Loyalty is when people are willing to turn down a better product or a better price to continue doing business with you. Loyal customers often don't even bother to research the competition or entertain other options. Loyalty is not easily won. Repeat business, however, is. All it takes is more manipulations.

Manipulative techniques have become such a mainstay in American business today that it has become virtually impossible for some to kick the habit. Like any addiction, the drive is not to get sober, but to find the next fix faster and more frequently. And as good as the short-term highs may feel, they have a deleterious impact on the long-term health of an organization. Addicted to the short-term results, business today has largely become a series of quick fixes added on one after another after another. The short-term tactics have become so sophisticated that an entire economy has developed to service the manipulations, equipped with statistics and quasi-science. Direct marketing companies, for example, offer calculations about which words will get the best results on each piece of direct mail they send out.

Those that offer mail-in rebates know the incentive works and they know that the higher the rebate, the more effective it is. They also know the cost that goes along with those rebates. To make them profitable, manufacturers rely on the breakage and slippage numbers staying above a certain threshold. Just like our trusty drug addict, whose behavior is reinforced by how good the short-term high feels, the temptation to make the qualifications of the rebate more obscure or cumbersome so as to reduce the number of qualified applicants can be overwhelming for some.

Samsung, the electronics giant, mastered the art of the kind of fine print that makes rebates so profitable for companies. In the early 2000s, the company offered rebates up to $150 on a variety of electronic products, stipulating in the fine print that the rebate was limited to one per address—a requirement that would have sounded reasonable enough to anyone at the time. Yet in practice, it effectively disqualified all customers who lived in apartment buildings where more than one resident had applied for the same rebate. More than 4,000 Samsung customers lured by the cash back received notices denying them rebates on those grounds. The practice was brought to the attention of the New York attorney general, and in 2004 Samsung was ordered to pay $200,000 in rebate claims to apartment dwellers. This is an extreme case of a company that got caught. But the rebate game of cutting out UPC symbols, filling out forms and doing it all before the deadline is alive and well. How can a company claim to be customer-focused when they are so comfortable measuring the number of customers who will fail to realize any promise of savings?

Manipulations Lead to Transactions, Not Loyalty

"It's simple," explains the TV infomercial, "simply put your old gold jewelry in the prepaid, insured envelope and we'll send you a check for the value of the gold in just two days." Mygoldenvelope .com is one of the leaders in this industry, serving as a broker for gold to be sent to a refinery, melted down, and reintroduced into the commodity market.

When Douglas Feirstein and Michael Moran started the company, they wanted to be the best in the business. They wanted to transform an industry with the reputation of a back-alley pawn shop and give it a bit of a Tiffany's sheen. They invested money in making the experience perfect. They worked to make the customer service experience ideal. They were both successful entrepreneurs and knew the value of building a brand and a strong customer experience. They'd spent a lot of money trying to get the balance right, and they made sure to explain their difference in direct response advertising on various local and national cable stations. "Better than the similar offers," they'd say. And they were right. But the investment didn't pay off as expected.

A few months later, Feirstein and Moran made a significant discovery: almost all of their customers did business with them only once. They had a transactional business yet they were trying to make it so much more than that. So they stopped trying to make their service "better than similar offers," and instead settled with good. Given that most people were not going to become repeat customers, there weren't going to be any head-to-head comparisons made to the other services. All they needed to do was drive a purchase decision and offer a pleasant enough experience that people would recommend it to a friend. Any more was unnecessary. Once the owners of mygoldenvelope.com realized they didn't need to invest in the things that build loyalty if all they wanted to do was drive transactions, their business became vastly more efficient and more profitable.

For transactions that occur an average of once, carrots and sticks are the best way to elicit the desired behavior. When the police offer a reward they are not looking to nurture a relationship with the witness or tipster; it is just a single transaction. When you lose your kitten and offer a reward to get it back, you don't need to have a lasting relationship with the person returning it; you just want your cat back.

Manipulations are a perfectly valid strategy for driving a transaction, or for any behavior that is only required once or on rare occasions. The rewards the police use are designed to incentivize witnesses to come forward to provide tips or evidence that may lead to an arrest. And, like any promotion, the manipulation will work if the incentive feels high enough to mitigate the risk.

In any circumstance in which a person or organization wants more than a single transaction, however, if there is a hope for a loyal, lasting relationship, manipulations do not help. Does a politician want your vote, for example, or does he or she want a lifetime of support and loyalty from you? (Judging by how elections are run these days, it seems all they want is to win elections. Ads discrediting opponents, a focus on single issues, and an uncomfortable reliance on fear or aspirational desires are all indicators. Those tactics win elections, but they do not seed loyalties among the voters.)

The American car industry learned the hard way the high cost of relying on manipulations to build a business when loyalty was what they really needed to nurture. While manipulations may be a viable strategy when times are good and money is flush, a change in market conditions made them too expensive. When the oil crisis of 2008 hit, the auto industry's promotions and incentives became untenable (the same thing happened in the 1970s). In this case, how long the manipulations could produce short-term gains was defined by the length of time the economy could sustain the strategy. This is a fundamentally weak platform upon which to build a business, an assumption of never-ending boom. Though loyal customers are less tempted by other offers and incentives, in good times the free flow of business makes it hard to recognize their value. It's in the tough times that loyal customers matter most.

Manipulations work, but they cost money. Lots of money. When the money is not as available to fund those tactics, not having a loyal following really hurts. After September 11, there were customers who sent checks to Southwest Airlines to show their support. One note that accompanied a check for $1,000 read, "You've been so good to me over the years, in these hard times I wanted to say thank you by helping you out." The checks that Southwest Airlines received were certainly not enough to make any significant impact on the company's bottom line, but they were symbolic of the feeling customers had for the brand. They had a sense of partnership. The loyal behavior of those who didn't send money is almost impossible to measure, but its impact has been invaluable over the long term, helping Southwest to maintain its position as the most profitable airline in history.

Knowing you have a loyal customer and employee base not only reduces costs, it provides massive peace of mind. Like loyal friends, you know your customers and employees will be there for you when you need them most. It is the feeling of "we're in this together," shared between customer and company, voter and candidate, boss and employee, that defines great leaders.

In contrast, relying on manipulations creates massive stress for buyer and seller alike. For the buyer, it has become increasingly difficult to know which product, service, brand or company is best. I joke about the proliferation of toothpaste varieties and the difficulty of choosing the right one. But toothpaste is just a metaphor. Nearly every decision we're asked to make every single day is like choosing toothpaste. Deciding what law firm to hire, college to attend, car to buy, company to work for, candidate to elect—there are just too many choices. All the advertising, promotions and pressure employed to tempt us one way or another, each attempting to push harder than the other to court us for our money or our support, ultimately yields one consistent result: stress.

For the companies too, whose obligation it is to help us decide, their ability to do so has gotten more and more difficult. Every day, the competition is doing something new, something better. To constantly have to come up with a new promotion, a new guerrilla marketing tactic, a new feature to add, is hard work. Combined with the long-term effects of years of short-term decisions that have eroded profit margins, this raises stress levels inside organizations as well. When manipulations are the norm, no one wins.

It's not an accident that doing business today, and being in the workforce today, is more stressful than it used to be. Peter Whybrow, in his book *American Mania: When More Is Not Enough*, argues that many of the ills that we suffer from today have very little to do with the bad food we're eating or the partially hydrogenated oils in our diet. Rather, Whybrow says, it's the way that corporate America has developed that has increased our stress to levels so high we're literally making ourselves sick because of it. Americans are suffering ulcers, depression, high blood pressure, anxiety, and cancer at record levels. According to Whybrow, all those promises of more, more, more are actually overloading the reward circuits of our brain. The short-term gains that drive business in America today are actually destroying our health.

Just Because It Works Doesn't Make It Right

The danger of manipulations is that they work. And because manipulations work, they have become the norm, practiced by the vast majority of companies and organizations, regardless of size or industry. That fact alone creates a systemic peer pressure. With perfect irony, we, the manipulators, have been manipulated by our own system. With every price drop, promotion, fear-based or aspirational message, and novelty we use to achieve our goals, we find our companies, our organizations and our systems getting weaker and weaker.

The economic crisis that began in 2008 is just another, albeit extreme, example of what can happen if a flawed assumption is allowed to carry on for too long. The collapse of the housing market and the subsequent collapse of the banking industry were due to decisions made inside the banks based on a series of manipulations. Employees were manipulated with bonuses that encouraged short-sighted decision-making. Open shaming of anyone who spoke out discouraged responsible dissent. A free flow of loans encouraged aspiring homebuyers to buy more than they could afford at all price levels. There was very little loyalty. It was all a series of transactional decisions—effective, but at a high cost. Few were working for the good of the whole. Why would they?—there was no reason given to do so. There was no cause or belief beyond instant gratification. Bankers weren't the first to be swept up by their own success. American car manufacturers have conducted themselves the same way for decades—manipulation after manipulation, short-term decision built upon short-term decision. Buckling or even collapse is the only logical conclusion when manipulations are the main course of action.

The reality is, in today's world, manipulations are the norm.

But there is an alternative.

PART 2

AN ALTERNATIVE
PERSPECTIVE

3

THE GOLDEN CIRCLE

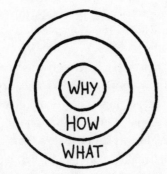

There are a few leaders who choose to inspire rather than manipulate in order to motivate people. Whether individuals or organizations, every single one of these inspiring leaders thinks, acts and communicates exactly the same way. And it's the complete opposite of the rest of us. Consciously or not, how they do it is by following a naturally occurring pattern that I call The Golden Circle.

The concept of The Golden Circle was inspired by the golden ratio—a simple mathematical relationship that has fascinated mathematicians, biologists, architects, artists, musicians and naturists since the beginning of history. From the Egyptians to Pythagoras to Leonardo da Vinci, many have looked to the golden ratio to provide a mathematical formula for proportion and even beauty. It also supports the notion that there is more order in nature than we think, as in the symmetry of leaves and the geometric perfection of snowflakes.

What I found so attractive about the golden ratio, however, was that it had so many applications in so many fields. And even more significantly, it offered a formula that could produce repeatable and predictable results in places where such results might have been assumed to be a random occurrence or luck. Even Mother Nature—for most people a symbol of unpredictability—exhibited more order than we previously acknowledged. Like the golden ratio, which offers evidence of order in the seeming disorder of nature, The Golden Circle finds order and predictability in human behavior. Put simply, it helps us understand why we do what we do. The Golden Circle provides compelling evidence of how much more we can achieve if we remind ourselves to start everything we do by first asking why.

The Golden Circle is an alternative perspective to existing assumptions about why some leaders and organizations have achieved such a disproportionate degree of influence. It offers clear insight as to how Apple is able to innovate in so many diverse industries and never lose its ability to do so. It explains why people tattoo Harley-Davidson logos on their bodies. It provides a clearer understanding not just of how Southwest Airlines created the most profitable airline in history, but why the things it did worked. It even gives some clarity as to why people followed Dr. Martin Luther King Jr. in a movement that changed a nation and why we took up John F. Kennedy's challenge to put a man on the moon even after he died. The Golden Circle shows how these leaders were able to inspire action instead of manipulating people to act.

This alternative perspective is not just useful for changing the world; there are practical applications for the ability to inspire, too. It can be used as a guide to vastly improving leadership, corporate culture, hiring, product development, sales, and marketing. It even explains loyalty and how to create enough momentum to turn an idea into a social movement.

And it all starts from the inside out. It all starts with Why.

Before we can explore its applications, let me first define the terms, starting from the outside of the circle and moving inward.

WHAT: Every single company and organization on the planet knows WHAT they do. This is true no matter how big or small, no matter what industry. Everyone is easily able to describe the products or services a company sells or the job function they have within that system. WHATs are easy to identify.

HOW: Some companies and people know HOW they do WHAT they do. Whether you call them a "differentiating value proposition," "proprietary process" or "unique selling proposition," HOWs are often given to explain how something is different or better. Not as obvious as WHATs, many think these are the differentiating or motivating factors in a decision. It would be false to assume that's all that is required. There is one missing detail:

WHY: Very few people or companies can clearly articulate WHY they do WHAT they do. When I say WHY, I don't mean to make money—that's a result. By WHY I mean what is your purpose, cause or belief? WHY does your company exist? WHY do you get out of bed every morning? And WHY should anyone care?

When most organizations or people think, act or communicate they do so from the outside in, from WHAT to WHY. And for good reason—they go from clearest thing to the fuzziest thing. We say WHAT we do, we sometimes say HOW we do it, but we rarely say WHY we do WHAT we do.

But not the inspired companies. Not the inspired leaders. Every single one of them, regardless of their size or their industry, thinks, acts and communicates from the inside out.

I use Apple Inc. frequently as an example simply because they have broad recognition and their products are easy to grasp and compare to others. What's more, Apple's success over time is not typical. Their ability to remain one of the most innovative companies year after year, combined with their uncanny ability to attract a cultlike following, makes them a great example to demonstrate many of the principles of The Golden Circle.

I'll start with a simple marketing example.

If Apple were like most other companies, a marketing message from them would move from the outside in of The Golden Circle. It would start with some statement of WHAT the company does or makes, followed by HOW they think they are different or better than the competition, followed by some call to action. With that, the company would expect some behavior in return, in this case a purchase. A marketing message from Apple, if they were like everyone else, might sound like this:

We make great computers.
They're beautifully designed, simple to use and user-friendly.
Wanna buy one?

It's not a very compelling sales pitch, but that's how most companies sell to us. This is the norm. First they start with WHAT they do—"Here's our new car." Then they tell us how they do it or how they are better—"It's got leather seats, great gas mileage, and great financing." And then they make a call to action and expect a behavior.

You see this pattern in business-to-consumer markets as well as business-to-business environments: "Here's our law firm. Our lawyers went to the best schools and we represent the biggest clients. Hire us." This pattern is also alive and well in politics—"Here's the candidate, here are her views on taxes and immigration. See how's she's different? Vote for her." In every case, the communication is organized in an attempt to convince someone of a difference or superior value.

But that is not what the inspiring leaders and organizations do. Every one of them, regardless of size or industry, thinks, acts and communicates from the inside out.

Let's look at that Apple example again and rewrite the example in the order Apple *actually* communicates. This time, the example starts with WHY.

> Everything we do, we believe in challenging the status quo. We believe in thinking differently.
> The way we challenge the status quo is by making our products beautifully designed, simple to use and user-friendly.
> And we happen to make great computers.
> Wanna buy one?

It's a completely different message. It actually *feels* different from the first one. We're much more eager to buy a computer from Apple after reading the second version—and all I did was reverse the order of the information. There's no trickery, no manipulation, no free stuff, no aspirational messages, no celebrities.

Apple doesn't simply reverse the order of information, their message starts with WHY, a purpose, cause or belief that has nothing to do with WHAT they do. WHAT they do—the products they make, from computers to small electronics—no longer serves as the reason to buy, they serve as the tangible proof of their cause. The design and user interface of Apple products, though important, are not enough in themselves to generate such astounding loyalty among their customers. Those important elements help make the cause tangible and rational. Others can hire top designers and brilliant engineers and make beautiful, easy-to-use products and copy the things Apple does, and they could even steal away Apple employees to do it, but the results would not be the same. Simply copying WHAT Apple does or HOW it does it won't work. There is something more, something hard to describe and near impossible to copy that gives Apple such a disproportionate level of influence in the market. The example starts to prove that people don't buy WHAT you do, they buy WHY you do it.

It's worth repeating: people don't buy WHAT you do, they buy WHY you do it.

Apple's ability to design such innovative products so consistently and their ability to command such astounding loyalty for their products comes from more than simply WHAT they do. The problem is, organizations use the tangible features and benefits to build a rational argument for why their company, product or idea is better than another. Sometimes those comparisons are made outright and sometimes analogies or metaphors are drawn, but the effect is the same. Companies try to sell us WHAT they do, but we buy WHY they do it. This is what I mean when I say they communicate from the outside in; they lead with WHAT and HOW.

When communicating from the inside out, however, the WHY is offered as the reason to buy and the WHATs serve as the tangible proof of that belief. The things we can point to rationalize or explain the reasons we're drawn to one product, company or idea over another.

WHAT companies do are external factors, but WHY they do it is something deeper. In practical terms, there is nothing special about Apple. It is just a company like any other. There is no real difference between Apple and any of its competitors—Dell, HP, Gateway, Toshiba. Pick one, it doesn't matter. They are all corporate structures. That's all a company is. It's a structure. They all make computers. They all have some systems that work and some that don't. They all have equal access to the same talent, the same resources, the same agencies, the same consultants and the same media. They all have some good managers, some good designers and smart engineers. They all make some products that work well and some that don't . . . even Apple. Why, then, does Apple have such a disproportionate level of success? Why are they more innovative? Why are they consistently more profitable? And how did they manage to build such a cultish loyal following—something very few companies are ever able to achieve?

People don't buy WHAT you do, they buy WHY you do it. This is the reason Apple has earned a remarkable level of flexibility. People are obviously comfortable buying a computer from Apple. But people are also perfectly comfortable buying an mp3 player from them, or a cell phone or a DVR. Consumers and investors are completely at ease with Apple offering so many different products in so many different categories. It's not WHAT Apple does that distinguishes them. It is WHY they do it. Their products give life to their cause.

I'm not so foolhardy as to propose that their products don't matter; of course they do. But it's the reason they matter that is contrary to the conventional wisdom. Their products, unto themselves, are not the reason Apple is perceived as superior; their products, WHAT Apple makes, serve as the tangible proof of what they believe. It is that clear correlation between WHAT they do and WHY they do it that makes Apple stand out. This is the reason we perceive Apple as being authentic. Everything they do works to demonstrate their WHY, to challenge the status quo. Regardless of the products they make or industry in which they operate, it is always clear that Apple "thinks different."

When Apple first came out with the Macintosh, having an operating system based on a graphical user interface and not a complicated computer language challenged how computers worked at the time. What's more, where most technology companies saw their biggest marketing opportunity among businesses, Apple wanted to give an individual sitting at home the same power as any company. Apple's WHY, to challenge the status quo and to empower the individual, is a pattern in that it repeats in all they say and do. It comes to life in their iPod and even more so in iTunes, a service that challenged the status quo of the music industry's distribution model and was better suited to how individuals consumed music.

The music industry was organized to sell albums, a model that evolved during a time when listening to music was largely an activity we did at home. Sony changed that in 1979 with the introduction of the Walkman. But even the Walkman, and later the Discman, was limited to the number of cassette tapes or CDs you could carry in addition to the device. The development of the mp3 music format changed all that. Digital compression allowed for a very high quantity of songs to be stored on relatively inexpensive and highly portable digital music devices. Our ability to walk out of the house with only one easy-to-carry device transformed music into something we largely listened to away from home. And the mp3 not only changed where we listened to music, it also transformed us from an album-collecting culture to a song-collecting culture. While the music industry was still busy trying to sell us albums, a model that no longer suited consumer behavior, Apple introduced their iPod by offering us "1,000 songs in your pocket." With the iPod and iTunes, Apple did a much better job of communicating the value of both the mp3 and the mp3 player relative to how we lived our lives. Their advertising didn't offer exhaustive descriptions of product details; it wasn't about them, it was about us. And we understood WHY we wanted it.

Apple did not invent the mp3, nor did they invent the technology that became the iPod, yet they are credited with transforming the music industry with it. The multigigabyte portable hard drive music player was actually invented by Creative Technology Ltd., a Singapore-based technology company that rose to prominence by making the Sound Blaster audio technology that enables home PCs to have sound. In fact, Apple didn't introduce the iPod until twenty-two months after Creative's entry into the market. This detail alone calls into question the assumption of a first mover's advantage. Given their history in digital sound, Creative was more qualified than Apple to introduce a digital music product. The problem was, they advertised their product as a "5GB mp3 player." It is exactly the same message as Apple's "1,000 songs in your pocket." The difference is Creative told us WHAT their product was and Apple told us WHY we needed it.

Only later, once we decided we had to have an iPod, did the WHAT matter—and we chose the 5GB version, 10GB version, and so on, the tangible details that proved we could get the 1,000 songs in our pocket. Our decision started with WHY, and so did Apple's offering.

How many of us can say with certainty that, indeed, an iPod is actually better than Creative's Zen? iPods, for example, are still plagued with battery life and battery replacement issues. They tend to just die. Maybe a Zen is better. The reality is, we don't even care if it is. People don't buy WHAT you do, they buy WHY you do it. And it is Apple's clarity of WHY that gives them such a remarkable ability to innovate, often competing against companies seemingly more qualified than they, and succeed in industries outside their core business.

The same cannot be said for companies with a fuzzy sense of WHY. When an organization defines itself by WHAT it does, that's all it will ever be able to do. Apple's competitors, having defined themselves by their products or services, regardless of their "differentiating value proposition," are not afforded the same freedom. Gateway, for example, started selling flat-screen TVs in 2003. Having made flat-screen monitors for years, they were every bit as qualified to make and sell TVs. But the company failed to make a credible name for itself among consumer electronics brands and gave up the business two years later to focus on its "core business." Dell came out with PDAs in 2002 and mp3 players in 2003, but lasted only a few years in each market. Dell makes good-quality products and is fully qualified to produce these other technologies. The problem was they had defined themselves by WHAT they did; they made computers, and it simply didn't make sense to us to buy a PDA or mp3 player from them. It didn't feel right. How many people do you think would stand on line for six hours to buy a new cell phone from Dell, as they did for the release of Apple's iPhone? People couldn't see Dell as anything more than a computer company. It just didn't make sense. Poor sales quickly ended Dell's desire to enter the small electronic goods market; instead they opted to "focus on their core business." Unless Dell, like so many others, can rediscover their founding purpose, cause or belief and start with WHY in all they say and do, all they will ever do is sell computers. They will be stuck in their "core business."

Apple, unlike its competitors, has defined itself by WHY it does things, not WHAT it does. It is not a computer company, but a company that challenges the status quo and offers individuals simpler alternatives. Apple even changed its legal name in 2007 from Apple Computer, Inc. to Apple Inc. to reflect the fact that they were more than just a computer company. Practically speaking, it doesn't really matter what a company's legal name is. For Apple, however, having the word "Computer" in their name didn't limit WHAT they could do. It limited how they thought of themselves. The change wasn't practical, it was philosophical.

Apple's WHY was formed at its founding in the late 1970s and hasn't changed to this date. Regardless of the products they make or the industries into which they migrate, their WHY still remains a constant. And Apple's intention to challenge accepted thinking has proved prophetic. As a computer company they redirected the course of the personal computing industry. As a small electronics company they have challenged the traditional dominance of companies like Sony and Philips. As a purveyor of mobile phones they pushed the old hands—Motorola, Ericsson, and Nokia—to reexamine their own businesses. Apple's ability to enter and even dominate so many different industries has even challenged what it means to be a computer company in the first place. Regardless of WHAT it does, we know WHY Apple exists.

The same cannot be said for their competitors. Although they all had a clear sense of WHY at some point—it was one of the primary factors that helped each of them become billion-dollar companies—over the course of time, all of Apple's competitors lost their WHY. Now all those companies define themselves by WHAT they do: we make computers. They turned from companies with a cause into companies that sold products. And when that happens, price, quality, service and features become the primary currency to motivate a purchase decision. At that point a company and its products have ostensibly become commodities. As any company forced to compete on price, quality, service or features alone can attest, it is very hard to differentiate for any period of time or build loyalty on those factors alone. Plus it costs money and is stressful waking up every day trying to compete on that level alone. Knowing WHY is essential for lasting success and the ability to avoid being lumped in with others.

Any company faced with the challenge of how to differentiate themselves in their market is basically a commodity, regardless of WHAT they do or HOW they do it. Ask a milk producer, for example, and they will tell you that there are actually variations among milk brands. The problem is you have to be an expert to understand the differences. To the outside world, all milk is basically the same, so we just lump all the brands together and call it a commodity. In response, that's how the industry acts. This is largely the pattern for almost every other product or service on the market today, business-to-consumer or business-to-business. They focus on WHAT they do and HOW they do it without consideration of WHY; we lump them together and they act like commodities. The more we treat them like commodities, the more they focus on WHAT and HOW they do it. It's a vicious cycle. But only companies that act like commodities are the ones who wake up every day with the challenge of how to differentiate. Companies and organizations with a clear sense of WHY never worry about it. They don't think of themselves as being like anyone else and they don't have to "convince" anyone of their value. They don't need complex systems of carrots and sticks. They *are* different, and everyone knows it. They start with WHY in everything they say and do.

There are those who still believe that Apple's difference comes from its marketing ability. Apple "sells a lifestyle," marketing professionals will tell you. Then how come these marketing professionals haven't intentionally repeated Apple's success and longevity for another company? Calling it a "lifestyle" is a recognition that people who live a certain way choose to incorporate Apple into their lives. Apple didn't invent the lifestyle, nor does it sell a lifestyle. Apple is simply one of the brands that those who live a certain lifestyle are drawn to. Those people use certain products or brands in the course of living in that lifestyle; that is, in part, how we recognize their way of life in the first place. The products they choose become proof of WHY they do the things they do. It is only because Apple's WHY is so clear that those who believe what they believe are drawn to them. As Harley-Davidson fits into the lifestyle of a certain group of people and Prada shoes fit the lifestyle of another group, it is the lifestyle that came first. Like the products the company produces that serve as proof of the company's WHY, so too does a brand or product serve as proof of an individual's WHY.

Others, even some who work for Apple, will say that what truly distinguishes Apple is in fact the quality of their products alone. Having good-quality products is of course important. No matter how clear your WHY, if WHAT you sell doesn't work, the whole thing falls flat. But a company doesn't need to have the best products, they just need to be good or very good. Better or best is a relative comparison. Without first understanding WHY, the comparison itself is of no value to the decision maker.

The concept of "better" begs the question: based on what standard? Is a Ferrari F430 sports car better than a Honda Odyssey minivan? It depends why you need the car. If you have a family of six, a two-seater Ferrari is not better. However, if you're looking for a great way to meet women, a Honda minivan is probably not better (depending on what kind of woman you're looking to meet, I guess; I too shouldn't make assumptions). Why the product exists must first be considered and why someone wants it must match. I could tell you about all the engineering marvels of the Honda Odyssey, some of which may actually be better than a Ferrari. It certainly gets better gas mileage. The odds are that I'm not going to convince someone who really wants that sports car to buy anything else. That some people are viscerally drawn to a Ferrari more than a Honda Odyssey says more about the person than the engineering of the product. The engineering, for example, would simply be one of the tangible points that a Ferrari lover could point out to prove how he feels about the car. The dogged defense of the superiority of the Ferrari from the person whose personality is predisposed to favor all the features and benefits of a Ferrari cannot be an objective conversation. Why do you think most people who buy Ferraris are willing to pay a premium to get it in red whereas most who buy Honda Odysseys probably don't care much about the color at all?

For all those who will try to convince you that Apple computers are just better, I cannot dispute a single claim. All I can offer is that most of the factors that they believe make them better meet their standard of what a computer should do. With that in mind, Macintoshes are, in practice, only better for those who believe what Apple believes. Those people who share Apple's WHY believe that Apple's products are objectively better, and any attempt to convince them otherwise is pointless. Even with objective metrics in hand, the argument about which is better or which is worse without first establishing a common standard creates nothing more than debate. Loyalists for each brand will point to various features and benefits that matter to them (or don't matter to them) in an attempt to convince the other that they are right. And that's one of the primary reasons why so many companies feel the need to differentiate in the first place—based on the flawed assumption that only one group can be right. But what if both parties were right? What if an Apple was right for some people and a PC was right for others? It's not a debate about better or worse anymore, it's a discussion about different needs. And before the discussion can even happen, the WHYs for each must be established first.

A simple claim of better, even with the rational evidence to back it up, can create desire and even motivate a decision to buy, but it doesn't create loyalty. If a customer feels inspired to buy a product, rather than manipulated, they will be able to verbalize the reasons why they think what they bought is better. Good quality and features matter, but they are not enough to produce the dogged loyalty that all the most inspiring leaders and companies are able to command. It is the cause that is represented by the company, brand, product or person that inspires loyalty.

Not the Only Way, Just One Way

Knowing your WHY is not the only way to be successful, but it is the only way to maintain a lasting success and have a greater blend of innovation and flexibility. When a WHY goes fuzzy, it becomes much more difficult to maintain the growth, loyalty and inspiration that helped drive the original success. By difficult, I mean that manipulation rather than inspiration fast becomes the strategy of choice to motivate behavior. This is effective in the short term but comes at a high cost in the long term.

Consider the classic business school case of the railroads. In the late 1800s, the railroads were the biggest companies in the country. Having achieved such monumental success, even changing the landscape of America, remembering WHY stopped being important to them. Instead they became obsessed with WHAT they did—they were in the railroad business. This narrowing of perspective influenced their decision-making—they invested all their money in tracks and crossties and engines. But at the beginning of the twentieth century, a new technology was introduced: the airplane. And all those big railroad companies eventually went out of business. What if they had defined themselves as being in the mass transportation business? Perhaps their behavior would have been different. Perhaps they would have seen opportunities that they otherwise missed. Perhaps they would own all the airlines today.

The comparison raises the question of the long-term survivability of so many other companies that have defined themselves and their industries by WHAT they do. They have been doing it the same way for so long that their ability to compete against a new technology or see a new perspective becomes a daunting task. The story of the railroads has eerie similarities to the case of the music industry discussed earlier. This is another industry that has not done a good job of adjusting its business model to fit a behavioral change prompted by a new technology. But other industries whose business models evolved in a different time show similar cracks—the newspaper, publishing and television industries, to name but three. These are the current-day railroads that are struggling to define their value while watching their customers turn to companies from other industries to serve their needs. Perhaps if music companies had a clearer sense of WHY, they would have seen the opportunity to invent the equivalent of iTunes instead of leaving it to a scrappy computer company.

In all cases, going back to the original purpose, cause or belief will help these industries adapt. Instead of asking, "WHAT should we do to compete?" the questions must be asked, "WHY did we start doing WHAT we're doing in the first place, and WHAT can we do to bring our cause to life considering all the technologies and market opportunities available today?" But don't take my word for it. None of this is my opinion. It is all firmly grounded in the tenets of biology.

4

THIS IS NOT OPINION, THIS IS BIOLOGY

Now, the Star-Belly Sneetches had bellies with stars.
The Plain-Belly Sneetches had none upon thars.
Those stars weren't so big. They were really so small.
You might think such a thing wouldn't matter at all.

Then, quickly, Sylvester McMonkey McBean
Put together a very peculiar machine.
And he said, "You want stars like a Star-Belly Sneetch?
My friends, you can have them for three dollars each!"

In his 1961 story about the Sneetches, Dr. Seuss introduced us to two groups of Sneetches, one with stars on their bellies and the other with none. The ones without stars wanted desperately to get stars so they could feel like they fit in. They were willing to go to extreme lengths and pay larger and larger sums of money simply to feel like they were part of a group. But only Sylvester McMonkey McBean, the man whose machine puts "stars upon thars," profited from the Sneetches' desire to fit in.

As with so many things, Dr. Seuss explained it best. The Sneetches perfectly capture a very basic human need—the need to belong. Our need to belong is not rational, but it is a constant that exists across all people in all cultures. It is a feeling we get when those around us share our values and beliefs. When we feel like we belong we feel connected and we feel safe. As humans we crave the feeling and we seek it out.

Sometimes our feeling of belonging is incidental. We're not friends with everyone from our hometown, but travel across the state, and you may meet someone from your hometown and you instantly have a connection with them. We're not friends with everyone from our home state, but travel across the country, and you'll feel a special bond with someone you meet who is from your home state. Go abroad and you'll form instant bonds with other Americans you meet. I remember a trip I took to Australia. One day I was on a bus and heard an American accent. I turned and struck up a conversation. I immediately felt connected to them, we could speak the same language, understand the same slang. As a stranger in a strange city, for that brief moment, I felt like I belonged, and because of it, I trusted those strangers on the bus more than any other passengers. In fact, we spent time together later. No matter where we go, we trust those with whom we are able to perceive common values or beliefs.

Our desire to feel like we belong is so powerful that we will go to great lengths, do irrational things and often spend money to get that feeling. Like the Sneetches, we want to be around people and organizations who are like us and share our beliefs. When companies talk about WHAT they do and how advanced their products are, they may have appeal, but they do not necessarily represent something to which we want to belong. But when a company clearly communicates their WHY, what they believe, and we believe what they believe, then we will sometimes go to extraordinary lengths to include those products or brands in our lives. This is not because they are better, but because they become markers or symbols of the values and beliefs we hold dear. Those products and brands make us feel like we belong and we feel a kinship with others who buy the same things. Fan clubs, started by customers, are often formed without any help from the company itself. These people form communities, in person or online, not just to share their love of a product with others, but to be in the company of people like them. Their decisions have nothing to do with the company or its products; they have everything to do with the individuals themselves.

Our natural need to belong also makes us good at spotting things that don't belong. It's a sense we get. A feeling. Something deep inside us, something we can't put into words, allows us to feel how some things just fit and some things just don't. Dell selling mp3 players just doesn't feel right because Dell defines itself as a computer company, so the only things that belong are computers. Apple defines itself as a company on a mission and so anything they do that fits that definition feels like it belongs. In 2004, they produced a promotional iPod in partnership with the iconoclastic Irish rock band U2. That makes sense. They would never have produced a promotional iPod with Celine Dion, even though she's sold vastly more records than U2 and may have a bigger audience. U2 and Apple belong together because they share the same values and beliefs. They both push boundaries. It would not have made sense if Apple released a special iPod with Celine Dion. As big as her audience may be, the partnership just doesn't align.

Look no farther than Apple's TV commercials "I'm a Mac and I'm a PC" for a perfect representation of who a Mac user needs to be to feel like they belong. In the commercial, the Mac user is a young guy, always in jeans and a T-shirt, always relaxed and always having a sense of humor poking fun at "the system." The PC, as defined by Apple, is in a suit. Older. Stodgy. To fit in with Mac, you have to be like Mac. Microsoft responded to Apple with its own "I'm a PC" campaign, which depicts people from all walks of life identifying themselves as "PC." Microsoft included many more people in their ads—teachers, scientists, musicians and children. As one would expect from the company that supplies 95 percent of the computer operating systems, to belong to that crowd, you have to be everyone else. One is not better or worse; it depends on where you feel like you belong. Are you a rabble-rouser or are you with the majority?

We are drawn to leaders and organizations that are good at communicating what they believe. Their ability to make us feel like we belong, to make us feel special, safe and not alone is part of what gives them the ability to inspire us. Those whom we consider great leaders all have an ability to draw us close and to command our loyalty. And we feel a strong bond with those who are also drawn to the same leaders and organizations. Apple users feel a bond with each other. Harley riders are bonded to each other. Anyone who was drawn to hear Dr. Martin Luther King Jr. give his "I Have a Dream" speech, regardless of race, religion or sex, stood together in that crowd as brothers and sisters, bonded by their shared values and beliefs. They knew they belonged together because they could feel it in their gut.

Gut Decisions Don't Happen in Your Stomach

The principles of The Golden Circle are much more than a communications hierarchy. Its principles are deeply grounded in the evolution of human behavior. The power of WHY is not opinion, it's biology. If you look at a cross section of the human brain, from the top down, you see that the levels of The Golden Circle correspond precisely with the three major levels of the brain.

The newest area of the brain, our *Homo sapien* brain, is the

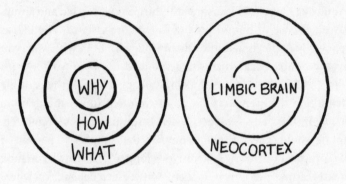

neocortex, which corresponds with the WHAT level. The neocortex is responsible for rational and analytical thought and language.

The middle two sections comprise the limbic brain. The limbic brain is responsible for all of our feelings, such as trust and loyalty. It is also responsible for all human behavior and all our decision-making, but it has no capacity for language.

When we communicate from the outside in, when we communicate WHAT we do first, yes, people can understand vast amounts of complicated information, like facts and features, but it does not drive behavior. But when we communicate from the inside out, we're talking directly to the part of the brain that controls decision-making, and our language part of the brain allows us to rationalize those decisions.

The part of the brain that controls our feelings has no capacity for language. It is this disconnection that makes putting our feelings into words so hard. We have trouble, for example, explaining why we married the person we married. We struggle to put into words the real reasons why we love them, so we talk around it or rationalize it. "She's funny, she's smart," we start. But there are lots of funny and smart people in the world, but we don't love them and we don't want to marry them. There is obviously more to falling in love than just personality and competence. Rationally, we know our explanation isn't the real reason. It is how our loved ones make us feel, but those feelings are really hard to put into words. So when pushed, we start to talk around it. We may even say things that don't make any rational sense. "She completes me," we might say, for example. What does that mean and how do you look for someone who does that so you can marry them? That's the problem with love; we only know when we've found it because it "just feels right."

The same is true for other decisions. When a decision feels right, we have a hard time explaining why we did what we did. Again, the part of the brain that controls decision-making doesn't control language, so we rationalize. This complicates the value of polls or market research. Asking people why they chose you over another may provide wonderful evidence of how they have rationalized the decision, but it does not shed much light on the true motivation for the decision. It's not that people don't know, it's that they have trouble explaining why they do what they do. Decision-making and the ability to explain those decisions exist in different parts of the brain.

This is where "gut decisions" come from. They just feel right. There is no part of the stomach that controls decision-making, it all happens in the limbic brain. It's not an accident that we use that word "feel" to explain those decisions either. The reason gut decisions feel right is because the part of the brain that controls them also controls our feelings. Whether you defer to your gut or you're simply following your heart, no matter which part of the body you think is driving the decision, the reality is it's all in your limbic brain.

Our limbic brain is powerful, powerful enough to drive behavior that sometimes contradicts our rational and analytical understanding of a situation. We often trust our gut even if the decision flies in the face of all the facts and figures. Richard Restak, a well-known neuroscientist, talks about this in his book *The Naked Brain*. When you force people to make decisions with only the rational part of their brain, they almost invariably end up "overthinking." These rational decisions tend to take longer to make, says Restak, and can often be of lower quality. In contrast, decisions made with the limbic brain, gut decisions, tend to be faster, higher-quality decisions. This is one of the primary reasons why teachers tell students to go with their first instinct when taking a multiple-choice test, to trust their gut. The more time spent thinking about the answer, the bigger the risk that it may be the wrong one. Our limbic brains are smart and often know the right thing to do. It is our inability to verbalize the reasons that may cause us to doubt ourselves or trust the empirical evidence when our gut tells us not to.

Consider the experience of buying a flat-screen TV at your local electronics store. You stand in the aisle listening to an expert explain to you the difference between LCD and plasma. The sales rep gives you all the rational differences and benefits, yet you are still none the wiser as to which one is best for you. After an hour, you still have no clue. Your mind is on overload because you're overthinking the decision. You eventually make a choice and walk out of the store, still not 100 percent convinced you chose the right one. Then you go to your friend's house and see that he bought the "other one." He goes on and on about how much he loves his TV. Suddenly you're jealous, even though you still don't know that his is any better than yours. You wonder, "Did I buy the wrong one?"

Companies that fail to communicate a sense of WHY force us to make decisions with only empirical evidence. This is why those decisions take more time, feel difficult or leave us uncertain. Under these conditions manipulative strategies that exploit our desires, fears, doubts or fantasies work very well. We're forced to make these less-than-inspiring decisions for one simple reason—companies don't offer us anything else besides the facts and figures, features and benefits upon which to base our decisions. Companies don't tell us WHY.

People don't buy WHAT you do, they buy WHY you do it. A failure to communicate WHY creates nothing but stress or doubt. In contrast, many people who are drawn to buy Macintosh computers or Harley-Davidson motorcycles, for example, don't need to talk to anyone about which brand to choose. They feel the utmost confidence in their decision and the only question they ask is which Mac or which Harley. At that level, the rational features and benefits, facts and figures absolutely matter, but not to drive the decision to give money or loyalty to the company or brand. That decision is already made. The tangible features are simply to help direct the choice of product that best fits our needs. In these cases, the decisions happened in the perfect inside-out order. Those decisions started with WHY—the emotional component of the decision—and then the rational components allowed the buyer to verbalize or rationalize the reasons for their decision.

This is what we mean when we talk about winning hearts and minds. The heart represents the limbic, feeling part of the brain, and the mind is the rational, language center. Most companies are quite adept at winning minds; all that requires is a comparison of all the features and benefits. Winning hearts, however, takes more work. Given the evidence of the natural order of decision-making, I can't help but wonder if the order of the expression "hearts and minds" is a coincidence. Why does no one set out to win "minds and hearts"?

The ability to win hearts before minds is not easy. It's a delicate balance of art and science—another coincidental grammatical construction. Why is it that things are not a balance of science and art, but always art before science? Perhaps it is a subtle clue our language-impaired limbic brain is sending us to help us see that the art of leading is about following your heart. Perhaps our brains are trying to tell us that WHY must come first.

Absent a WHY, a decision is harder to make. And when in doubt we look to science, to data, to guide decisions. Companies will tell you that the reason they start with WHAT they do or HOW they do it is because that's what their customers asked for. Quality. Service. Price. Features. That's what the data reported. But for the fact that the part of the brain that controls decision-making is different from the part of the brain that is able to report back that decision, it would be a perfectly valid conclusion to give people what they ask for. Unfortunately, there is more evidence that sales don't significantly increase and bonds of loyalty are not formed simply when companies say or do everything their customers want. Henry Ford summed it up best. "If I had asked people what they wanted," he said, "they would have said a faster horse."

This is the genius of great leadership. Great leaders and great organizations are good at seeing what most of us can't see. They are good at giving us things we would never think of asking for. When the computer revolution was afoot, computer users couldn't ask for a graphical user interface. But that's what Apple gave us. In the face of expanding competition in the airline industry, most air travelers would never have thought to ask for less instead of more. But that's what Southwest did. And in the face of hard times and overwhelming odds, few would have asked their country, what can I do for you over what can you do for me? The very cause upon which John F. Kennedy introduced his presidency. Great leaders are those who trust their gut. They are those who understand the art before the science. They win hearts before minds. They are the ones who start with WHY.

We make decisions all day long, and many of them are emotionally driven. Rarely do we sift through all the available information to ensure we know every fact. And we don't need to. It is all about degrees of certainty. "I can make a decision with 30 percent of the information," said former secretary of state Colin Powell. "Anything more than 80 percent is too much." There is always a level at which we trust ourselves or those around us to guide us, and don't always *feel* we need all the facts and figures. And sometimes we just may not trust ourselves to make a certain decision yet. This may explain why we *feel* (there's that word again) so uncomfortable when others twist our arm to make a decision that doesn't sit well in our gut. We trust our gut to help us decide whom to vote for or which shampoo to buy. Because our biology complicates our ability to verbalize the real reasons why we make the decisions we do, we rationalize based on more tangible factors, like the design or the service or the brand. This is the basis for the false assumption that price or features matter more than they do. Those things matter, they provide us the tangible things we can point to to rationalize our decision-making, but they don't set the course and they don't inspire behavior.

It's What You Can't See That Matters

"Gets your whites whiter and your brights brighter," said the TV commercial for the newest laundry detergent. This was the value proposition for so many years in the laundry detergent business. A perfectly legitimate claim. That's what the market research revealed customers wanted. The data was true, but the truth of what people wanted was different.

The makers of laundry detergent asked consumers WHAT they wanted from detergent, and consumers said whiter whites and brighter brights. Not such a remarkable finding, if you think about it, that people doing laundry wanted their detergent to help get their clothes not just clean, but very clean. So brands attempted to differentiate HOW they got your whites whiter and brights brighter by trying to convince consumers that one additive was more effective than another. Protein, said one brand. Color enhancers, said another. No one asked customers WHY they wanted their clothes clean. That little nugget wasn't revealed until many years later when a group of anthropologists hired by one of the packaged-goods companies revealed that all those additives weren't in fact driving behavior. They observed that when people took their washing out of the dryer, no one held it up to the light to see how white it was or compared it to newer items to see how bright it was. The first thing people did when they pulled their laundry out of the dryer was to smell it. This was an amazing discovery. *Feeling* clean was more important to people than being clean. There was a presumption that all detergents get your clothes clean. That's what detergent is supposed to do. But having their clothes smell fresh and clean mattered much more than the nuanced differences between which detergent actually made clothes measurably cleaner.

That a false assumption swayed an entire industry to follow the wrong direction is not unique to detergents. Cell phone companies believed people wanted more options and buttons until Apple introduced its iPhone with fewer options and only one button. The German automakers believed their engineering alone mattered to American car buyers. They were stunned and perplexed when they learned that great engineering wasn't enough. One by one, the German luxury car makers begrudgingly added cup holders to their fine automobiles. It was a feature that mattered a great deal to commuter-minded Americans, but was rarely mentioned in any research about what factors influenced purchase decisions. I am not, for a moment, proposing that cup holders make people loyal to BMWs. All I am proposing is that even for rationally minded car buyers, there is more to decision-making than meets the eye. Literally.

The power of the limbic brain is astounding. It not only controls our gut decisions, but it can influence us to do things that seem illogical or irrational. Leaving the safety of home to explore faraway places. Crossing oceans to see what's on the other side. Leaving a stable job to start a business out of your basement with no money in the bank. Many of us look at these decisions and say, "That's stupid, you're crazy. You could lose everything. You could get yourself killed. What are you thinking?" It is not logic or facts but our hopes and dreams, our hearts and our guts, that drive us to try new things.

If we were all rational, there would be no small businesses, there would be no exploration, there would be very little innovation and there would be no great leaders to inspire all those things. It is the undying belief in something bigger and better that drives that kind of behavior. But it can also control behavior born out of other emotions, like hate or fear. Why else would someone plot to hurt someone they had never met?

The amount of market research that reveals that people want to do business with the company that offers them the best-quality products, with the most features, the best service and all at a good price is astounding. But consider the companies with the greatest loyalty—they rarely have all those things. If you wanted to buy a custom Harley-Davidson, you used to wait six months for delivery (to give them credit, they've got it down from a year). That's bad service! Apple's computers are at least 25 percent more expensive than a comparable PC. There is less software available for their operating system. They have fewer peripherals. The machines themselves are sometimes slower than a comparable PC. If people made only rational decisions, and did all the research before making a purchase, no one would ever buy a Mac. But of course people do buy Macs. And some don't just buy them—they love them, a feeling that comes straight from the heart. Or the limbic brain.

We all know someone who is a die-hard Mac lover. Ask them WHY they love their Mac. They won't tell you, "Well, I see myself as someone who likes to challenge the status quo, and it's important for me to surround myself with the people, products and brands that prove to the outside world who I believe I am." Biologically, that's what happened. But that decision was made in the part of the brain that controls behavior but not language. So they will provide a rationalization: "It's the user interface. It's the simplicity. It's the design. It's the high quality. They're the best computers. I'm a creative person." In reality, their purchase decision and their loyalty are deeply personal. They don't really care about Apple; it's all about them.

The same can even be said for the people who love to work at Apple. Even employees can't put it into words. In their case, their job is one of the WHATs to their WHY. They too are convinced it's the quality of the products alone that is behind Apple's success. But deep inside, they all love being a part of something bigger than themselves. The most loyal Apple employees, like the most loyal Apple customers, all love a good revolution. A great raise and added benefits couldn't convince a loyal Apple employee to work for Dell, and no amount of cash-back incentives and rebates could convince a loyal Mac user to switch to a PC (many are already paying double the price). This is beyond rational. This is a belief. It's no accident that the culture at Apple is often described as a cult. It's more than just products, it's a cause to support. It's a matter of faith.

Remember the Honda and the Ferrari? Products are not just symbols of what the company believes, they also serve as symbols of what the loyal buyers believe. People with Apple laptop computers, for example, love opening them up while sitting in an airport. They like that everyone knows they are using a Mac. It's an emblem, a symbol of who they are. That glowing Apple logo speaks to something about them and how they see the world. Does anyone notice when someone pops open the lid of their HP or Dell computer? No! Not even the people using the computers care. HP and Dell have a fuzzy sense of WHY, so their products and their brands don't symbolize anything about the users. To the Dell or HP user, their computer, no matter how fast or sleek, is not a symbol of a higher purpose, cause or belief. It's just a computer. In fact, for the longest time, the logo on the lid of a Dell computer faced the user so when they opened it, it would be upside down for everyone else.

Products with a clear sense of WHY give people a way to tell the outside world who they are and what they believe. Remember, people don't buy WHAT you do, they buy WHY you do it. If a company does not have a clear sense of WHY then it is impossible for the outside world to perceive anything more than WHAT the company does. And when that happens, manipulations that rely on pushing price, features, service or quality become the primary currency of differentiation.

5

CLARITY, DISCIPLINE
AND CONSISTENCY

Nature abhors a vacuum. In order to promote life, Mother Nature
attempts to find balance whenever possible. When life is destroyed
because of a forest fire, for example, nature will introduce new life
to replace it. The existence of a food chain in any ecosystem, in
which each animal exists as food for another, is a way of maintaining balance. The Golden Circle, grounded in natural principles of
biology, obeys the need for balance as well. As I've discussed, when
the WHY is absent, imbalance is produced and manipulations
thrive. And when manipulations thrive, uncertainty increases for
buyers, instability increases for sellers and stress increases for all.

Starting with WHY is just the beginning. There is still work to
be done before a person or an organization earns the right or ability to inspire. For The Golden Circle to work, each of the pieces
must be in balance and in the right order.

Clarity of WHY

It all starts with clarity. You have to know WHY you do WHAT you
do. If people don't buy WHAT you do, they buy WHY you do it, so
it follows that if you don't know WHY you do WHAT you do, how

will anyone else? If the leader of the organization can't clearly articulate WHY the organization exists in terms beyond its products or services, then how does he expect the employees to know WHY to come to work? If a politician can't articulate WHY she seeks public office beyond the standard "to serve the people" (the minimum rational standard for all politicians), then how will the voters know whom to follow? Manipulations can motivate the outcome of an election, but they don't help choose who should lead. To lead requires those who willingly follow. It requires those who believe in something bigger than a single issue. To inspire starts with the clarity of WHY.

Discipline of HOW

Once you know WHY you do what you do, the question is HOW will you do it? HOWs are your values or principles that guide HOW to bring your cause to life. HOW we do things manifests in the systems and processes within an organization and the culture. Understanding HOW you do things and, more importantly, having the discipline to hold the organization and all its employees accountable to those guiding principles enhances an organization's ability to work to its natural strengths. Understanding HOW gives greater ability, for example, to hire people or find partners who will naturally thrive when working with you.

Ironically, the most important question with the most elusive answer—WHY do you do what you do?—is actually quite simple and efficient to discover (and I'll share it in later chapters). It's the discipline to never veer from your cause, to hold yourself accountable to HOW you do things; that's the hardest part. Making it even more difficult for ourselves, we remind ourselves of our values by writing them on the wall . . . as nouns. Integrity. Honesty. Innovation. Communication, for example. But nouns are not actionable. They are things. You can't build systems or develop incentives around those things. It's nearly impossible to hold people accountable to nouns.

"A little more innovation today if you would please, Bob." And if you have to write "honesty" on your wall to remind you to do it, then you probably have bigger problems anyway.

For values or guiding principles to be truly effective they have to be verbs. It's not "integrity," it's "always do the right thing." It's not "innovation," it's "look at the problem from a different angle." Articulating our values as verbs gives us a clear idea . . . we have a clear idea of how to act in any situation. We can hold each other accountable to measure them or even build incentives around them. Telling people to have integrity doesn't guarantee that their decisions will always keep customers' or clients' best interests in mind; telling them to always do the right thing does. I wonder what values Samsung had written on the wall when they developed that rebate that wasn't applicable to people living in apartment buildings.

The Golden Circle offers an explanation for long-term success, but the inherent nature of doing things for the long term often includes investments or short-term costs. This is the reason the discipline to stay focused on the WHY and remain true to your values matters so much.

Consistency of WHAT

Everything you say and everything you do has to prove what you believe. A WHY is just a belief. That's all it is. HOWs are the actions you take to realize that belief. And WHATs are the results of those actions—everything you say and do: your products, services, marketing, PR, culture and whom you hire. If people don't buy WHAT you do but WHY you do it, then all these things must be consistent. With consistency people will see and hear, without a shadow of a doubt, what you believe. After all, we live in a tangible world. The only way people will know what you believe is by the things you say and do, and if you're not consistent in the things you say and do, no one will know what you believe.

It is at the WHAT level that authenticity happens. "Authenticity" is that word so often bandied about in the corporate and political worlds. Everyone talks about the importance of being authentic. "You must be *authentic*," experts say. "All the trend data shows that people prefer to do business with *authentic* brands." "People vote for the *authentic* candidate." The problem is, that instruction is totally unactionable.

How do you go into somebody's office and say, "From now on, please, a little more authenticity." "That marketing piece you're working on," a CEO might instruct, "please make it a little more authentic." What do companies do to make their marketing or their sales or whatever they're doing authentic?

The common solution is hilarious to me. They go out and do customer research and they ask the customers, what would we have to tell you for us to be authentic? This entirely misses the point. You can't ask others what you have to do to be authentic. Being authentic means that you already know. What does a politician say when told to be "more authentic"? How does a leader act more "authentically"? Without a clear understanding of WHY, the instruction is completely useless.

What authenticity means is that your Golden Circle is in balance. It means that everything you say and everything you do you *actually* believe. This goes for management as well as the employees. Only when that happens can the things you say and do be viewed as authentic. Apple believed that its original Apple computer and its Macintosh challenged the dominant IBM DOS platforms. Apple believes its iPod and iTunes products are challenging the status quo in the music industry. And we all understand WHY Apple does what it does. It is because of that mutual understanding that we view those Apple products as authentic. Dell introduced mp3 players and PDAs in an attempt to enter the small electronics business. We don't know what Dell's WHY is, we have no certainty about what the company believes or WHY it produced those products beyond self-gain and a desire to capitalize on a new market segment. Those products are not authentic. It's not that Dell couldn't enter other markets—it certainly has the knowledge and ability to make good products—but its ability to do so without a clear understanding of WHY is what makes it much harder and much more expensive. Just producing high-quality products and marketing them does not guarantee success. Authenticity cannot be achieved without clarity of WHY. And authenticity matters.

Ask the best salesmen what it takes to be a great salesman. They will always tell you that it helps when you really believe in the product you're selling. What does *belief* have to do with a sales job? Simple. When salesmen actually believe in the thing they are selling, then the words that come out of their mouths are authentic. When belief enters the equation, passion exudes from the salesman. It is this authenticity that produces the relationships upon which all the best sales organizations are based. Relationships also build trust. And with trust comes loyalty. Absent a balanced Golden Circle means no authenticity, which means no strong relationships, which means no trust. And you're back at square one selling on price, service, quality or features. You are back to being like everyone else. Worse, without that authenticity, companies resort to manipulation: pricing, promotions, peer pressure, fear, take your pick. Effective? Of course, but only for the short term.

Being authentic is not a requirement for success, but it is if you want that success to be a lasting success. Again, it goes back to WHY. Authenticity is when you say and do the things you actually believe. But if you don't know WHY the organization or the products exist on a level beyond WHAT you do, then it is impossible to know if the things you say or do are consistent with your WHY. Without WHY, any attempt at authenticity will almost always be inauthentic.

The Right Order

After you have clarity of WHY, are disciplined and accountable to your own values and guiding principles, and are consistent in all you say and do, the final step is to keep it all in the right order. Just like that little Apple marketing example I used earlier, simply changing the order of the information, starting with WHY, changed the impact of the message. The WHATs are important—they provide the tangible proof of the WHY—but WHY must come first. The WHY provides the context for everything else. As you will see over and over in all the cases and examples in this book, whether in leadership, decision-making or communication, starting with WHY has a profound and long-lasting impact on the result. Starting with WHY is what inspires people to act.

If You Don't Know WHY, You Can't Know HOW

Rollin King, a San Antonio businessman, hatched the idea to take what Pacific Southwest was doing in California and bring it to Texas—to start an airline that flew short-haul flights between Dallas, Houston and San Antonio. He had recently gone through a long and messy divorce and turned to the one man he trusted to help him get his idea off the ground. His Wild Turkey–drinking, chain-smoking divorce lawyer, Herb Kelleher.

In nearly every way, King and Kelleher were opposites. King, a numbers guy, was notoriously gruff and awkward, while Kelleher was gregarious and likable. At first Kelleher called King's idea a dumb one, but by the end of the evening King had successfully inspired him with his vision and Kelleher agreed to consider coming on board. It would take four years, however, before Southwest Airlines would make its first flight from Dallas's Love Field to Houston.

Southwest did not invent the concept of a low-cost airline. Pacific Southwest Airlines pioneered the industry—Southwest even copied their name. Southwest had no first mover's advantage—Braniff International Airways, Texas International Airlines and Continental Airlines were already serving the Texas market, and none was eager to give up any ground. But Southwest was not built to be an airline. It was built to champion a cause. They just happened to use an airline to do it.

In the early 1970s, only 15 percent of the traveling population traveled by air. At that rate, the market was small enough to scare off most would-be competitors to the big airlines. But Southwest wasn't interested in competing against everyone else for 15 percent of the traveling population. Southwest cared about the other 85 percent. Back then, if you asked Southwest whom their competition was, they would have told you, "We compete against the car and the bus." But what they meant was, "We're the champion for the common man." That was WHY they started the airline. That was their cause, their purpose, their reason for existing. HOW they went about building their company was not a strategy developed by a high-priced management consultancy. It wasn't a collection of best practices that they saw other companies doing. Their guiding principles and values stemmed directly from their WHY and were more common sense than anything else.

In the 1970s, air travel was expensive, and if Southwest was going to be the champion for the common man, they had to be cheap. It was an imperative. And in a day and age when air travel was elitist—back then people wore ties on planes—as the champion for the common man, Southwest had to be fun. It was an imperative. In a time when air travel was complicated, with different prices depending on when you booked, Southwest had to be simple. If they were to be accessible to the other 85 percent, then simplicity was an imperative. At the time, Southwest had two price categories: nights/weekends and daytime. That was it.

Cheap, fun and simple. That's HOW they did it. That's how they were to champion the cause of the common man. The result of their actions was made tangible in the things they said and did—their product, the people they hired, their culture and their marketing. "You are now free to move about the country," they said in their advertising. That's much more than a tagline. That's a cause. And it's a cause looking for followers. Those who could relate to Southwest, those who saw themselves as average Joes, now had an alternative to the big airlines. And those who believed what Southwest believed became fiercely loyal to the company. They felt Southwest was a company that spoke directly to them and directly for them. More importantly, they felt that flying Southwest said something about who they were as people. The loyalty that developed with their customers had nothing to do with price. Price was simply one of the ways the airline brought their cause to life.

Howard Putnam, one of the former presidents of Southwest, likes to tell a story of a senior executive of a large company who approached him after an event. The executive said he always flew one of the big airlines when he traveled on business. He had to, it was a company mandate. And although he had accumulated many frequent flier miles on the other airline and money was no object, when he flew for himself or with his family, he always flew Southwest. "He loves Southwest," Putnam says with a grin when he tells the story. Just because Southwest is cheap doesn't mean it only appeals to those with less money. Cheap is just one of the things Southwest does that helps us understand what they believe.

What Southwest has achieved is the stuff of business folklore. As a result of WHY they do what they do, and because they are highly disciplined in HOW they do it, they are the most profitable airline in history. There has never been a year that they didn't turn a profit, including after September 11 and during the oil crises of the 1970s and early 2000s. Everything Southwest says and does is authentic. Everything about them reflects the original cause King and Kelleher set out to champion decades earlier. It has never veered.

Fast-forward about thirty years. United Airlines and Delta Air Lines looked at the success of Southwest and decided they needed a low-cost product to compete and share in Southwest's success. "We got to get us one of those," they thought. In April 2003, Delta launched their low-cost alternative, Song. Less than a year later United launched Ted. In both cases, they copied HOW Southwest did it. They made Ted and Song cheap, fun and simple. And for anyone who ever flew Ted or Song, they were cheap, they were fun and they were simple. But both failed.

United and Delta were both old hands in the airline business and were every bit qualified to add whatever products they wanted to adapt to market conditions or seize opportunities. The problem was not with WHAT they did, the problem was, no one knew WHY Song or Ted existed. They may have even been better than Southwest. But it didn't matter. Sure, people flew them, but there are always reasons people do business with you that have nothing to do with you. That people can be motivated to use your product is not the issue; the problem was that too few were loyal to the brands. Without a sense of WHY, Song and Ted were just another couple of airlines. Without a clear sense of WHY, all that people had to judge them on was price or convenience. They were commodities that had to rely on manipulations to build their businesses, an expensive proposition. United abandoned its entry into the low-cost airline business just four years after it began, and Delta's Song also took its last flight only four years after it launched.

It is a false assumption that differentiation happens in HOW and WHAT you do. Simply offering a high-quality product with more features or better service or a better price does not create difference. Doing so guarantees no success. Differentiation happens in WHY and HOW you do it. Southwest isn't the best airline in the world. Nor are they always the cheapest. They have fewer routes than many of their competition and don't even fly outside the continental United States. WHAT they do is not always significantly better. But WHY they do it is crystal clear and everything they do proves it. There are many ways to motivate people to do things, but loyalty comes from the ability to inspire people. Only when the WHY is clear and when people believe what you believe can a true loyal relationship develop.

Manipulation and Inspiration Are Similar, but Not the Same

Manipulation and inspiration both tickle the limbic brain. Aspirational messages, fear or peer pressure all push us to decide one way or another by appealing to our irrational desires or playing on our fears. But it's when that emotional feeling goes deeper than insecurity or uncertainty or dreams that the emotional reaction aligns with how we view ourselves. It is at that point that behavior moves from being motivated to inspired. When we are inspired, the decisions we make have more to do with who we are and less to do with the companies or the products we're buying.

When our decisions *feel* right, we're willing to pay a premium or suffer an inconvenience for those products or services. This has nothing to do with price or quality. Price, quality, features and service are important, but they are the cost of entry in business today. It is those visceral limbic feelings that create loyalty. And it is that loyalty that gives Apple or Harley-Davidson or Southwest Airlines or Martin Luther King or any other great leader who commands a following such a huge advantage. Without a strong base of loyal followers, the pressure increases to manipulate—to compete or "differentiate" based on price, quality, service or features. Loyalty, real emotional value, exists in the brain of the buyer, not the seller.

It's hard to make a case to someone that your products or services are important in their lives based on external rational factors that *you* have defined as valuable (remember the Ferrari versus the Honda). However, if your WHYs and their WHY correspond, then they will see your products and services as tangible ways to prove what *they* believe. When WHY, HOW, and WHAT are in balance, authenticity is achieved and the buyer feels fulfilled. When they are out of balance, stress or uncertainty exists. When that happens, the decisions we make will also be out of balance. Without WHY, the buyer is easily motivated by aspiration or fear. At that point, it is the buyer who is at the greatest risk of ending up being inauthentic. If they buy something that doesn't clearly embody their own sense of WHY, then those around them have little evidence to paint a clear and accurate picture of who they are.

The human animal is a social animal. We're very good at sensing subtleties in behavior and judging people accordingly. We get good feelings and bad feelings about companies, just as we get good feelings and bad feelings about people. There are some people we just feel we can trust and others we just feel we can't. Those feelings also manifest when organizations try to court us. Our ability to feel one way or another toward a person or an organization is the same. What changes is who is talking to us, but it is always a single individual who is listening. Even when a company airs its message on TV, for example, no matter how many people see the commercial, it is always and only an individual that can receive the message. This is the value of The Golden Circle; it provides a way to communicate consistent with how individuals receive information. For this reason an organization must be clear about its purpose, cause or belief and make sure that everything they say and do is consistent with and authentic to that belief. If the levels of The Golden Circle are in balance, all those who share the organization's view of the world will be drawn to it and its products like a moth to a light bulb.

Doing Business Is Like Dating

I'd like to introduce you to our imaginary friend Brad. Brad is going on a date tonight. It's a first date and he's pretty excited. He thinks the woman he's about to meet is really beautiful and that she makes a great prospect. Brad sits down for dinner and he starts talking.

"I am extremely rich."
"I have a big house and I drive a beautiful car."
"I know lots of famous people."
"I'm on TV all the time, which is good because I'm good-looking."
"I've actually done pretty well for myself."

The question is, does Brad get a second date?

The way we communicate and the way we behave is all a matter of biology. That means we can make some comparisons between the things we do in our social lives and the things we do in our professional lives. After all, people are people. To learn how to apply WHY to a business situation, you needn't look much farther than how we act on a date. Because, in reality, there is no difference between sales and dating. In both circumstances, you sit across a table from someone and hope to say enough of the right things to close the deal. Of course, you could always opt for a manipulation or two, a fancy dinner, dropping hints of tickets that you have or whom you know. Depending on how badly you want to close the deal, you could tell them anything they want to hear. Promise them the world and the odds are good that you will close the deal. Once. Maybe twice. With time, however, maintaining that relationship will cost more and more. No matter the manipulations you choose, this is not the way to build a trusting relationship.

In Brad's case, it is obvious that the date did not go well. The odds are not good that he will get a second date, and he's certainly not done a good job of laying down the foundation to build a relationship. Ironically, the woman's initial interest may have been generated based on those elements. She agreed to go on the date because her friends told her that Brad was good-looking and that he had a good job and that he knew a lot of famous people. Even though all those things may be true, WHATs don't drive decision-making, WHATs should be used as proof of WHY, and the date plainly fell flat.

Let's send Brad out again, but this time he's going to start with WHY.

"You know what I love about my life?" he starts this time. "I get to wake up every day to do something I love. I get to inspire people to do the things that inspire them. It's the most wonderful thing in the world. In fact, the best part is trying to figure out all the different ways I can do that. It really is amazing. And believe it or not, I've actually been able to make a lot of money from it. I bought a big house and a nice car. I get to meet lots of famous people and I get to be on TV all the time, which is fun, because I'm good-looking. I'm very lucky that I'm doing something that I love, I've actually been able to do pretty well because of it."

This time the chances Brad will get a second date, assuming that whoever is sitting across from him believes what he believes, went up exponentially. More importantly, he's also laying a good foundation for a relationship, one based on values and beliefs. He said all the same things as on the first date; the only difference is he started with WHY, and all the WHATs, all the tangible benefits, served as proof of that WHY.

Now consider how most companies do business. Someone sits down across a table from you, they've heard you're a good prospect, and they start talking.

"Our company is extremely successful."

"We have beautiful offices, you should stop by and check them out sometime."

"We do business with all the biggest companies and brands."

"I'm sure you've seen our advertising."

"We're actually doing pretty well."

In business, like a bad date, many companies work so hard to prove their value without saying WHY they exist in the first place. You'll have to do more than show your résumé before someone finds you appealing, however. But that is exactly what companies do. They provide you with a long list of their experience—WHAT they've done, whom they know—all with the idea that you will find them so desirable that you will have to drop everything to do business with them.

People are people and the biology of decision-making is the same no matter whether it is a personal decision or a business decision. It's obvious that in the dating scenario it was a bad date, so why would we expect it to be any different in the business scenario?

Like on a date, it is exceedingly difficult to start building a trusting relationship with a potential customer or client by trying to convince them of all the rational features and benefits. Those things are important, but they serve only to give credibility to a sales pitch and allow buyers to rationalize their purchase decision. As with all decisions, people don't buy WHAT you do, they buy WHY you do it, and WHAT you do serves as the tangible proof of WHY you do it. But unless you start with WHY, all people have to go on are the rational benefits. And chances are you won't get a second date.

Here's the alternative:

"You know what I love about our company? Every single one of us comes to work every day to do something we love. We get to inspire people to do the things that inspire them. It's the most wonderful thing in the world. In fact, the fun part is trying to figure out all the different ways we can do that. It really is amazing. The best part is, it is also good for business. We do really well. We have beautiful offices, you should stop by sometime to see. We work with some of the biggest companies. I'm sure you've seen our ads. We're actually doing pretty well."

Now, how certain are you that the second pitch was better than the first?

Three Degrees of Certainty

When we can only provide a rational basis for a decision, when we can only point to tangible elements or rational measurements, the highest level of confidence we can give is, "I *think* this is the right decision." That would be biologically accurate because we're activating the neocortex, the "thinking" part of our brain. At a neocortical level we can verbalize our thoughts. This is what's happening when we spend all that time sifting through the pros and cons, listening to all the differences between plasma or LCD, Dell versus HP.

When we make gut decisions, the highest level of confidence we can offer is, "The decision *feels* right," even if it flies in the face of all the facts and figures. Again, this is biologically accurate, because gut decisions happen in the part of the brain that controls our emotions, not language. Ask the most successful entrepreneurs and leaders what their secret is and invariably they all say the same thing: "I trust my gut." The times things went wrong, they will tell you, "I listened to what others were telling me, even though it didn't feel right. I should have trusted my gut." It's a good strategy, except it's not scalable. The gut decision can only be made by a single person. It's a perfectly good strategy for an individual or a small organization, but what happens when success necessitates that more people be able to make decisions that *feel* right?

That's when the power of WHY can be fully realized. The ability to put a WHY into words provides the emotional context for decisions. It offers greater confidence than "I think it's right." It's more scalable than "I feel it's right." When you know your WHY, the highest level of confidence you can offer is, "I *know* it's right." When you *know* the decision is right, not only does it feel right, but you can also rationalize it and easily put it into words. The decision is fully balanced. The rational WHATs offer proof for the feeling of WHY. If you can verbalize the feeling that drove the gut decision, if you can clearly state your WHY, you'll provide a clear context for those around you to understand why that decision was made. If the decision is consistent with the facts and figures, then those facts and figures serve to reinforce the decision—this is balance. And if the decision flies in the face of all the facts and figures then it will highlight the other factors that need to be considered. It can turn a controversial decision from a debate into a discussion.

My former business partner, for example, would get upset when I turned away business. I would tell him that a potential client didn't "feel" right. That would frustrate him to no end because "the client's money was as good as everyone else's," he would tell me. He couldn't understand the reason for my decision, and worse, I couldn't explain it. It was just a feeling I had. In contrast, these days I can easily explain WHY I'm in business—to inspire people to do the things that inspire them. If I were to make the same decision now for the same gut reason, there is no debate because everyone is clear WHY the decision was made. We turn away business because those potential clients don't believe what we believe and they are not interested in anything to do with inspiring people. With a clear sense of WHY, a debate to take on a bad-fit client turns into a discussion of whether the imbalance is worth the short-term gain they may give us.

The goal of business should not be to do business with anyone who simply wants what you have. It should be to focus on the people who believe what you believe. When we are selective about doing business only with those who believe in our WHY, trust emerges.

PART 3

LEADERS NEED A FOLLOWING

6

THE EMERGENCE OF TRUST

To say that most of the company's employees were embarrassed to work there was an understatement. It was no secret that the employees felt mistreated. And if a company mistreats their people, just watch how the employees treat their customers. Mud rolls down a hill, and if you're the one standing at the bottom, you get hit with the full brunt. In a company, that's usually the customer. Throughout the 1980s, this was life at Continental Airlines—the worst airline in the industry.

"I could see Continental's biggest problem the second I walked in the door in February of 1994," Gordon Bethune wrote in *From Worst to First*, the chief executive's firsthand account of Continental's turnaround. "It was a crummy place to work." Employees were "surly to customers, surly to each other, and ashamed of their company. And you can't have a good product without people who like coming to work. It just can't be done," he recounts.

Herb Kelleher, the head of Southwest for twenty years, was considered a heretic for positing the notion that it is a company's responsibility to look after the employees first. Happy employees ensure happy customers, he said. And happy customers ensure happy shareholders—in that order. Fortunately, Bethune shared this heretical belief.

Some would argue that the reason Continental's culture was so poisonous was that the company was struggling. They would tell you that it's hard for executives to focus on anything other than survival when a company is facing hard times. "Once we get profitable again," the logic went, "then we will take a look at everything else." And without a doubt, throughout the 1980s and early 1990s, Continental struggled. The company filed for Chapter 11 bankruptcy protection twice in eight years—once in 1983 and again in 1991—and managed to go through ten CEOs in a decade. In 1994, the year Bethune took over as the newest CEO, the company had lost $600 million and ranked last in every measurable performance category.

But all that didn't last long once Bethune arrived. The very next year Continental made $250 million and was soon ranked as one of the best companies to work for in America. And while Bethune made significant changes to improve the operations, the greatest gains were in a performance category that is nearly impossible to measure: trust.

Trust does not emerge simply because a seller makes a rational case why the customer should buy a product or service, or because an executive promises change. Trust is not a checklist. Fulfilling all your responsibilities does not create trust. Trust is a feeling, not a rational experience. We trust some people and companies even when things go wrong, and we don't trust others even though everything might have gone exactly as it should have. A completed checklist does not guarantee trust. Trust begins to emerge when we have a sense that another person or organization is driven by things other than their own self-gain.

With trust comes a sense of value—real value, not just value equated with money. Value, by definition, is the transference of trust. You can't convince someone you have value, just as you can't convince someone to trust you. You have to earn trust by communicating and demonstrating that you share the same values and beliefs. You have to talk about your WHY and prove it with WHAT you do. Again, a WHY is just a belief, HOWs are the actions we take to realize that belief, and WHATs are the results of those actions. When all three are in balance, trust is built and value is perceived. This is what Bethune was able to do.

There are many talented executives with the ability to manage operations, but great leadership is not based solely on great operational ability. Leading is not the same as being the leader. Being the leader means you hold the highest rank, either by earning it, having good fortune or navigating internal politics. Leading, however, means that others willingly follow you—not because they have to, not because they are paid to, but because they want to. Frank Lorenzo, CEO before Bethune, may have been the leader of Continental, but Gordon Bethune knew how to lead the company. Those who lead are able to do so because those who follow trust that the decisions made at the top have the best interest of the group at heart. In turn, those who trust work hard because they feel like they are working for something bigger than themselves.

Prior to Bethune's arrival, the twentieth floor of the company's headquarters, the executive floor, was off-limits to most people. The executive suites were locked. Only those with a rank of senior vice president or higher were permitted to visit. Key cards were required to get onto the floor, security cameras were ubiquitous and armed guards roamed the floor to eliminate any doubt that the security was no joke. Clearly, the company suffered from trust issues. One story handed down was that Frank Lorenzo would not even drink a soda on a Continental plane if he didn't open the can himself. He didn't trust anyone, so it is no great leap of logic that no one trusted him. It's hard to lead when those whom you are supposed to be leading are not inclined to follow.

Bethune was very different. He understood that beyond the structure and systems a company is nothing more than a collection of people. "You don't lie to your own doctor," he says, "and you can't lie to your own employees." Bethune set out to change the culture by giving everyone something they could believe in. And what, specifically, did he give them to believe in that could turn the worst airline in the industry into the best airline in the industry with all the same people and all the same equipment?

In college I had a roommate named Howard Jeruchimowitz. Now an attorney in Chicago, Howard learned from an early age about a very simple human desire. Growing up in the suburbs of New York City, he played outfield on the worst team in the Little League. They lost nearly every game they played—and not by small margins either; they were regularly annihilated. Their coach was a good man and wanted to instill a positive attitude in the young athletes. After one of their more embarrassing losses, the coach pulled the team together and reminded them, "It doesn't matter who wins or loses, what matters is how you play the game." It was at this point that young Howard raised his hand and asked, "Then why do we keep score?"

Howard understood from a very young age the very human desire to win. No one likes to lose, and most healthy people live their life to win. The only variation is the score we use. For some it's money, for others it's fame or awards. For some it's power, love, a family or spiritual fulfillment. The metric is relative, but the desire is the same. A billionaire doesn't need to work. Money becomes a way to keep score—a relative account of how things are going. Even a billionaire who loses millions due to poor decisions can get depressed. Although the money may have zero impact on his lifestyle, no one likes to lose.

The drive to win is not, per se, a bad thing. Problems arise, however, when the metric becomes the only measure of success, when what you achieve is no longer tied to WHY you set out to achieve it in the first place.

Bethune set out to prove to everyone at Continental that if they wanted to win, they could win. And most of the employees stuck around to find out if he was right. There were a few exceptions. One executive who once held up a plane because he was running late was asked to leave, as were thirty-nine more of the top sixty executives who didn't believe. No matter how experienced they were or what they brought to the table, they were asked to leave if they weren't team players and weren't able to adapt to the new culture that Bethune was trying to build. There was no room for those who didn't believe in the new Continental.

Bethune knew that building a team to go out and win meant more than giving a few rah-rah speeches and bonuses for the top brass if they hit certain revenue targets. He knew that if he wanted to build a real, lasting success, people had to win not for him, not for the shareholders and not even for the customer. For the success to last the employees of Continental had to want to win for themselves.

Everything he talked about was in terms of how it benefited the employees. Instead of telling them to keep the planes clean for customers, he pointed out something more obvious. Every day they came to work on a plane. The passengers left after their flight, but many of the flight attendants had to stay on for at least one more trip. It's just nicer to come to work when the environment is cleaner.

Bethune also got rid of all the security on the twentieth floor. He instituted an open-door policy and made himself incredibly accessible. It was common for him to show up and sling bags with some of the baggage handlers at the airport. From now on, this was a family and everyone had to work together.

Bethune focused on the things they knew to be important, and to an airline the most important thing is to get the planes running on time. In the early 1990s, before Bethune arrived, Continental had the lowest on-time rating of the nation's ten largest airlines. So Bethune told employees that each month Continental's on-time percentage ranked in the top five, every employee would receive a check for $65. When you consider that Continental had 40,000 employees in 1995, every on-time month cost the airline a whopping $2.5 million, But Bethune knew he was getting a deal: being chronically late was costing it $5 million a month in expenses like missed connections and putting passengers up overnight. But most important to Bethune was what the bonus program did for the company culture: it got tens of thousands of employees, including managers, all pointed in the same direction for the first time in years.

Gone were the days when only the brass would enjoy the benefits of success. Everyone got their $65 when the airline did well and no one got it when the airline missed its targets. Bethune even insisted that a separate check be sent out. It wasn't just added to their salary check. This was different. This was a symbol of winning. And on every check a message reminded them WHY they came to work: "Thank you for helping make Continental one of the best."

"We measured things the employees could truly control," Bethune said. "We made the stakes something the employees would win or lose on together, not separately."

Everything they did made people feel like they were in it together. And they were.

The Only Difference Between You and a Caveman Is the Car You Drive

The reason the human race has been so successful is not because we're the strongest animals—far from it. Size and might alone do not guarantee success. We've succeeded as a species because of our ability to form cultures. Cultures are groups of people who come together around a common set of values and beliefs. When we share values and beliefs with others, we form trust. Trust of others allows us to rely on others to help protect our children and ensure our personal survival. The ability to leave the den to hunt or explore with confidence that the community will protect your family and your stuff until you return is one of the most important factors in the survival of an individual and the advancement of our species.

That we trust people with common values and beliefs is not, in itself, a profound assertion. There is a reason we're not friends with everyone we meet. We're friends with people who see the world the way we see it, who share our views and our belief set. No matter how good a match someone looks on paper, that doesn't guarantee a friendship. You can think of it on a macro scale also. The world is filled with different cultures. Being American is not better than being French. They are just different cultures—not better or worse, just different. American culture strongly values ideals of entrepreneurship, independence and self-reliance. We call our WHY—the American Dream. French culture strongly values ideals of unified identity, group reliance and joie de vivre. (Notice that we use the French word to describe the joy-of-life lifestyle. Coincidence? Perhaps.) Some people are good fits in French culture and some people are good fits in American culture. It is not a matter of better or worse, they are just different.

Most people who are born and raised in one culture will, for obvious reasons, end up being a reasonably good fit in that culture, but not always. There are people who grew up in France who never quite felt like they belonged; they were misfits in their own culture. So they moved, maybe to America. Drawn to the feelings they had for America's WHY, they followed the American Dream and emigrated.

It is always said that America is fueled in large part by immigrants. But it is completely false that all immigrants make productive members of a society. It's not true that all immigrants have an entrepreneurial spirit—just the ones that are viscerally drawn to America. That's what a WHY does. When it is clearly understood, it attracts people who believe the same thing. And assuming they are good fits for what Americans believe and how they do things, those immigrants will say of America, "I love it here," or "I love this country." This visceral reaction has less to do with America and more to do with them. It's how they feel about their own opportunity and their own ability to thrive in a culture in which they feel like they belong versus the one they came from.

And within the big WHY that is America, it breaks down even further. Some people are better fits in New York and some are better fits in Minneapolis. One culture is not better or worse than the other, they are just different. Many people dream of moving to New

York, for example, attracted to the glamour or the perception of opportunity. They arrive with aspirations of making it big, but they fail to consider whether they will fit into the culture before they make their move. Some make it. But so many don't. Over and over, I've seen people come to New York with big hopes and dreams, but either couldn't find the job they wanted or they found it but couldn't take the pressure. They are not dumb or bad or poor workers. They were just bad fits. They either stay in New York and exert more effort than they need to, hating their jobs and their lives, or they move. If they move to a city in which they are better fits—Chicago or San Francisco or somewhere else—they often end up much happier and more successful. New York is not rationally better than other cities, it's just not right for everyone. Like all cities, it's only right for those who are good fits.

The same can be said for any place that has a strong culture or recognizable personality. We do better in cultures in which we are good fits. We do better in places that reflect our own values and beliefs. Just as the goal is not to do business with anyone who simply wants what you have, but to do business with people who believe what you believe, so too is it beneficial to live and work in a place where you will naturally thrive because your values and beliefs align with the values and beliefs of that culture.

Now consider what a company is. A company is a culture. A group of people brought together around a common set of values and beliefs. It's not products or services that bind a company together. It's not size and might that make a company strong, it's the culture—the strong sense of beliefs and values that everyone, from the CEO to the receptionist, all share. So the logic follows, the goal is not to hire people who simply have a skill set you need, the goal is to hire people who believe what you believe.

Finding the People Who Believe What You Believe

Early in the twentieth century, the English adventurer Ernest Shackleton set out to explore the Antarctic. Roald Amundsen, a Norwegian, had only just become the first explorer ever to reach the South Pole, leaving one remaining conquest: the crossing of the continent via the southernmost tip of the earth.

The land part of the expedition would start at the frigid Weddell Sea, below South America, and travel 1,700 miles across the pole to the Ross Sea, below New Zealand. The cost, Shackleton estimated at the time, would be about $250,000. "The crossing of the south polar continent will be the biggest polar journey ever attempted," Shackleton told a reporter for the *New York Times* on December 29, 1913. "The unknown fields in the world which are still unconquered are narrowing down, but there still remains this great work."

On December 5, 1914, Shackleton and a crew of twenty-seven men set out for the Weddell Sea on the *Endurance*, a 350-ton ship that had been constructed with funds from private donors, the British government and the Royal Geographical Society. By then, World War I was raging in Europe, and money was growing more scarce. Donations from English schoolchildren paid for the dog teams.

But the crew of the *Endurance* would never reach the continent of Antarctica.

Just a few days out of South Georgia Island in the southern Atlantic, the ship encountered mile after mile of pack ice, and was soon trapped as winter moved in early and with fury. Ice closed in around the ship "like an almond in a piece of toffee," a crew member wrote. Shackleton and his crew were stranded in the Antarctic for ten months as the *Endurance* drifted slowly north, until the pressure of the ice floes finally crushed the ship. On November 21, 1915, the crew watched as she sank in the frigid waters of the Weddell Sea.

Stranded on the ice, the crew of the *Endurance* boarded their three lifeboats and landed on tiny Elephant Island. There Shackleton left behind all but five of his men and embarked on a hazardous journey across 800 miles of rough seas to find help. Which, eventually, they did.

What makes the story of the *Endurance* so remarkable, however, is not the expedition, it's that throughout the whole ordeal no one died. There were no stories of people eating others and no mutiny.

This was not luck. This was because Shackleton hired good fits. He found the right men for the job. When you fill an organization with good fits, those who believe what you believe, success just happens. And how did Shackleton find this amazing crew? With a simple ad in the London *Times*.

Compare that to how we hire people. Like Shackleton, we run ads in the newspaper, or on the modern equivalents, Craigslist or Monster.com. Sometimes we hire a recruiter to find someone for us, but the process is largely the same. We provide a list of qualifications for the job and expect that the best candidate will be the one who meets those requirements.

The issue is how we write those ads. They are all about WHAT and not about WHY. A want ad might say, for example, "Account executive needed, minimum five years' experience, must have working knowledge of industry. Come work for a fantastic, fast-growing company with great pay and great benefits." The ad may produce loads of applicants, but how do we know which is the right fit?

Shackleton's ad for crew members was different. His did not say WHAT he was looking for. His ad did not say:

"Men needed for expedition. Minimum five years' experience. Must know how to hoist mainsail. Come work for a fantastic captain."

Rather, Shackleton was looking for those with something more. He was looking for a crew that belonged on such an expedition. His actual ad ran like this:

"Men wanted for Hazardous journey. Small wages, bitter cold, long months of complete darkness, constant danger, safe return doubtful. Honour and recognition in case of success."

The only people who applied for the job were those who read the ad and thought it sounded great. They loved insurmountable odds. The only people who applied for the job were survivors. Shackleton hired only people who believed what he believed. Their ability to survive was guaranteed. When employees belong, they will guarantee your success. And they won't be working hard and looking for innovative solutions for you, they will be doing it for themselves.

What all great leaders have in common is the ability to find good fits to join their organizations—those who believe what they believe. Southwest Airlines is a great example of a company with a knack for hiring good fits. Their ability to find people who embody their cause makes it much easier for them to provide great service. As Herb Kelleher famously said, "You don't hire for skills, you hire for attitude. You can always teach skills." This is all fine and good; the problem is, which attitude? What if their attitude is not one that fits your culture?

I love asking companies whom they like to hire, and one of the most common answers I am given is, "We hire only passionate people." But how do you know if someone is passionate for interviewing, but not so passionate for working? The truth is, almost every person on the planet is passionate, we are just not all passionate for the same things. Starting with WHY when hiring dramatically increases your ability to attract those who are passionate for what you believe. Simply hiring people with a solid résumé or great work ethic does not guarantee success. The best engineer at Apple, for example, would likely be miserable if he worked at Microsoft. Likewise, the best engineer at Microsoft would probably not thrive at Apple. Both are highly experienced and work hard. Both may come highly recommended. However, each engineer does not fit the culture of the other's company. The goal is to hire those who are passionate for your WHY, your purpose, cause or belief, and who have the attitude that fits your culture. Once that is established, only then should their skill set and experience be evaluated. Shackleton could have had the most experienced crew money could buy, but if they weren't able to connect on a level much deeper than their ability, their survival would not have been a foregone conclusion.

For years, Southwest didn't have a complaints department— they didn't need one. Though Kelleher rightly talked about the need to hire for attitude, the airline in fact deserves more credit for hiring the good fits responsible for providing great service. Kelleher was not the only one making the hiring decisions, and asking everyone to simply trust their gut is too risky. Their genius came from figuring out why some people were such good fits and then developing systems to find more of them.

In the 1970s, Southwest Airlines decided to put their flight attendants in hot pants and go-go boots as part of their uniforms (hey, it was the 1970s). It wasn't their idea; Pacific Southwest, the California-based airline after which Southwest modeled itself, did it first, Southwest simply copied them. Unlike Pacific Southwest, however, Southwest figured out something that would prove invaluable. They realized that when they recruited flight attendants, the only people who applied for the job were cheerleaders and majorettes. That's because they were the only people who didn't mind wearing the new uniforms. Cheerleaders and majorettes, however, fit in perfectly at Southwest. They didn't just have a great attitude, their whole disposition was about cheering people on. Spreading optimism. Leading crowds to believe that "we can win." They were perfect fits at a company that was the champion of the common man. Realizing this, Southwest started to recruit only cheerleaders and majorettes.

Great companies don't hire skilled people and motivate them, they hire already motivated people and inspire them. People are either motivated or they are not. Unless you give motivated people something to believe in, something bigger than their job to work toward, they will motivate themselves to find a new job and you'll be stuck with whoever's left.

Give 'Em a Cathedral

Consider the story of two stonemasons. You walk up to the first stonemason and ask, "Do you like your job?" He looks up at you and replies, "I've been building this wall for as long as I can remember. The work is monotonous. I work in the scorching hot sun all day. The stones are heavy and lifting them day after day can be backbreaking. I'm not even sure if this project will be completed in my lifetime. But it's a job. It pays the bills." You thank him for his time and walk on.

About thirty feet away, you walk up to a second stonemason. You ask him the same question, "Do you like your job?" He looks up and replies, "I love my job. I'm building a cathedral. Sure, I've been working on this wall for as long as I can remember, and yes, the work is sometimes monotonous. I work in the scorching hot sun all day. The stones are heavy and lifting them day after day can be backbreaking. I'm not even sure if this project will be completed in my lifetime. But I'm building a cathedral."

WHAT these two stonemasons are doing is exactly the same; the difference is, one has a sense of purpose. He feels like he belongs. He comes to work to be a part of something bigger than the job he's doing. Simply having a sense of WHY changes his entire view of his job. It makes him more productive and certainly more loyal. Whereas the first stonemason would probably take another job for more pay, the inspired stonemason works longer hours and would probably turn down an easier, higher-paying job to stay and be a part of the higher cause. The second stonemason does not see himself as any more or less important than the guy making the stained glass windows or even the architect. They are all working together to build the cathedral. It is this bond that creates camaraderie. And that camaraderie and trust is what brings success. People working together for a common cause.

Companies with a strong sense of WHY are able to inspire their employees. Those employees are more productive and innovative, and the feeling they bring to work attracts other people eager to work there as well. It's not such a stretch to see why the companies that we love to do business with are also the best employers. When people inside the company know WHY they come to work, people outside the company are vastly more likely to understand WHY the company is special. In these organizations, from the management on down, no one sees themselves as any more or any less than anyone else. They all need each other.

When Motivated by WHY, Success Just Happens

It was a turn-of-the-century version of the dot-com boom. The promise of a revolutionary new technology was changing the way people imagined the future. And there was a race to see who could do it first. It was the end of the nineteenth century and the new technology was the airplane. One of the best-known men in the field was Samuel Pierpont Langley. Like many other inventors of his day, he was attempting to build the world's first heavier-than-air flying machine. The goal was to be the first to achieve machine-powered, controlled, manned flight. The good news was Langley had all the right ingredients for the enormous task; he had, what most would define as, the recipe for success.

Langley had achieved some renown within the academic community as an astronomer, which earned him high-ranking and prestigious positions. He was secretary of the Smithsonian Institution. He had been an assistant in the Harvard College Observatory and professor of mathematics at the United States Naval Academy. Langley was very well connected. His friends included some of the most powerful men in government and business, including Andrew Carnegie and Alexander Graham Bell. He was also extremely well funded. The War Department, the precursor the Department of Defense, had given him $50,000 for the project, a lot of money in those days. Money was no object.

Langley assembled some of the best and brightest minds of the day. His dream team included test pilot Charles Manly, a brilliant Cornell-trained mechanical engineer, and Stephan Balzer, the developer of the first car in New York. Langley and his team used the finest materials. The market conditions were perfect and his PR was great. The *New York Times* followed him around everywhere. Everyone knew Langley and was rooting for his success.

But there was a problem.

Langley had a bold goal, but he didn't have a clear sense of WHY. His purpose for wanting to build the plane was defined in terms of WHAT he was doing and WHAT he could get. He had had a passion for aeronautics since a very young age, but he did not have a cause to champion. More than anything else, Langley wanted to be first. He wanted to be rich and he wanted to be famous. That was his driving motivation.

Although already well regarded in his own field, he craved the kind of fame of a Thomas Edison or Alexander Graham Bell, the kind that comes only with inventing something big. Langley saw the airplane as his ticket to fame and fortune. He was smart and motivated. He had what we still assume is the recipe for success: plenty of cash, the best people and ideal market conditions. But few of us have ever heard of Samuel Pierpont Langley.

A few hundred miles away in Dayton, Ohio, Orville and Wilbur Wright were also building a flying machine. Unlike Langley, the Wright brothers did not have the recipe for success. Worse, they seemed to have the recipe for failure. There was no funding for their venture. No government grants. No high-level connections. The Wright brothers funded their dream with the proceeds from their bicycle shop. Not a single person working on the team, including Orville and Wilbur, had a college education; some did not even finish high school. What the Wright brothers were doing wasn't any different from Langley or all the others trying to build a flying machine. But the Wright brothers did have something very special. They had a dream. They knew WHY it was important to build this thing. They believed that if they could figure out this flying machine, it would change the world. They imagined the benefits to everyone else if they were successful.

"Wilbur and Orville were true scientists, deeply and genuinely concerned about the physical problem they were trying to solve—the problem of balance and flight," said James Tobin, the Wright brothers' biographer. Langley, on the other hand, was consumed with acquiring the level of prestige of his associates like Alexander

Graham Bell, fame that he knew would come only with a major scientific breakthrough. Langley, Tobin said, "did not have the Wrights' passion for flight, but rather was looking for achievement."

Orville and Wilbur preached what they believed and inspired others in the community to join them in their cause. The proof of their commitment was self-evident. With failure after failure, most would have given up, but not the Wright brothers' team. The team was so inspired that no matter how many setbacks they suffered they would show up for more. Every time the Wright brothers went out to make a test flight, so the stories go, they would take five sets of parts with them, because they knew that's how many times they were likely to fail before deciding to come home for the day.

Then it happened. On December 17, 1903, on a field in Kitty Hawk, North Carolina, the Wright brothers took to the sky. A fifty-nine-second flight at an altitude of 120 feet at the speed of a jog was all it took to usher in a new technology that would change the world.

Remarkable as the achievement was, it went relatively unnoticed. The *New York Times* was not there to cover the story. Driven by something bigger than fame and glory, the Wright brothers were content to wait to tell the world. They understood its true significance to the world.

What Langley and the Wright brothers were trying to create was exactly the same; both were building the same product. Both the Wright brothers and Langley were highly motivated. Both had a strong work ethic. Both had keen scientific minds. What the Wright brothers' team had that Langley didn't wasn't luck. It was inspiration. One was motivated by the prospect of fame and wealth, the other by a belief. The Wright brothers excited the human spirit of those around them. Langley paid for talent to help him get rich and famous. The Wright brothers started with WHY. Further proof Langley was motivated by WHAT: a short time after Orville and Wilbur took flight, Langley quit. He got out of the business. He could have said, "That's amazing, now I'm going to improve upon their technology." But he didn't. He found the defeat humiliating—

his own test flight had landed in the Potomac River, and the news-papers all made fun of him. He cared so much about what others thought of him, he was so preoccupied with becoming famous. He wasn't first, so he simply quit.

Innovation Happens at the Edges

Dream teams are not always so dreamy. When a team of experts comes together they often work for themselves and not for the good of the whole. This is what happens when companies feel the need to pay mega-salaries to "get the best talent." Those people are not necessarily showing up because they believe in your WHY, they are showing up for the money. A classic manipulation. Paying someone a lot of money and asking them to come up with great ideas ensures very little. However, pulling together a team of like-minded people and giving them a cause to pursue ensures a greater sense of teamwork and camaraderie. Langley pulled together a dream team and promised them riches. The Wright brothers in-spired a group of people to join them in pursuit of something big-ger than each member of the team. Average companies give their people something to work on. In contrast, the most innovative or-ganizations give their people something to work toward.

The role of a leader is not to come up with all the great ideas. The role of a leader is to create an environment in which great ideas can happen. It is the people inside the company, those on the front lines, who are best qualified to find new ways of doing things. The people who answer the phones and talk to customers, for ex-ample, can tell you more about the kinds of questions they get than can anyone sitting in an executive suite miles away. If the people inside a company are told to come to work and just do their job, that's all they will do. If they are constantly reminded WHY the company was founded and told to always look for ways to bring that cause to life while performing their job, however, then they will do more than their job.

Steve Jobs, for example, did not personally come up with the iPod or iTunes or the iPhone. Others inside the company did. Jobs gave people a filter, a context, a higher purpose around which to innovate: find existing status quo industries, those in which companies fight to protect their old-fashioned business models, and challenge them. This is WHY Apple was founded, it is what Jobs and Wozniak did when they started the company, and it is what Apple's people and products have done ever since. It's a repeating pattern. Apple's employees simply look for ways to bring their cause to life in as many places as they can. And it works.

It is not the same at many other companies. Companies that define themselves by WHAT they do instead of WHY they do it instruct their people to be innovative around a product or service. "Make it better," they are instructed. Those who work for Apple's competitors, companies that have defined themselves as "computer manufacturers," come to work to develop "more innovative" computers. The best they can do is add more RAM, add a feature or two, or, as one PC maker has done, give people the option to customize the color of their computer casing. This hardly qualifies as an idea with the potential to change the course of an industry. A nice feature, for sure, but not innovation. If you are curious as to how Colgate finds itself with thirty-two different types of toothpaste today, it is because every day its people come to work to develop a better toothpaste and not, for example, to look for ways to help people feel more confident about themselves.

Apple does not have a lock on good ideas; there are smart, innovative thinkers at most companies. But great companies give their people a purpose or challenge around which to develop ideas rather than simply instruct them to make a better mousetrap. Companies that study their competitors in hopes of adding the features and benefits that will make *their* products "better" are only working to entrench the company in WHAT it does. Companies with a clear sense of WHY tend to ignore their competition, whereas those with a fuzzy sense of WHY are obsessed with what others are doing.

The ability of a company to innovate is not just useful for developing new ideas, it is invaluable for navigating struggle. When people come to work with a higher sense of purpose, they find it easier to weather hard times or even to find opportunity in those hard times. People who come to work with a clear sense of WHY are less prone to giving up after a few failures because they understand the higher cause. Thomas Edison, a man definitely driven by a higher cause, said, "I didn't find a way to make a lightbulb, I found a thousand ways how not to make one."

Southwest Airlines is famous for pioneering the ten-minute turnaround—the ability to deplane, prep, and board a plane in ten minutes. This ability helps an airline make more money, because the more the planes are in the sky, the better the company is doing. What few people realize is that this innovation was born out of struggle. In 1971, Southwest was running low on cash and needed to sell one of their aircraft to stay in business. This left them with three planes to fly a schedule that required four. They had two choices: they could scale back their operations, or they could figure out how to turn their planes around in ten minutes. And thus was born the ten-minute turnaround.

Whereas most other airline employees would have simply said it couldn't be done, Southwest's people rallied to figure out how to perform the unprecedented and seemingly impossible task. Today, their innovation is still paying dividends. Because of increased airport congestion and larger planes and cargo loads, Southwest now takes about twenty-five minutes to turn their planes around. However, if they were to try to keep the same schedule but add even five minutes to the turnaround time, they would need an additional eighteen planes in their fleet at a cost of nearly a billion dollars.

Southwest's remarkable ability to solve problems, Apple's remarkable knack for innovation and the Wright brothers' ability to develop a technology with the team they had were all possible for the same reason: they believed they could and they trusted their people to do it.

The Definition of Trust

Founded by Sir Francis Baring in 1762, Barings Bank was the oldest merchant bank in England. The bank, which survived the Napoleonic Wars, World War I and World War II, was unable to survive the predilection for risk of one self-proclaimed rogue trader. Nick Leeson single-handedly brought down Barings Bank in 1995 by performing some unauthorized, extremely high-risk trades. Had the proverbial winds continued to blow in the right direction, Leeson would have made himself and the bank extremely rich and he would have been hailed as a hero.

But such is the nature of unpredictable things like the weather and financial markets. Few dispute that what Leeson was doing was anything more than gambling. And gambling is very different from calculated risk. Calculated risk accepts that there can be great loses, but steps are taken to either guard against or respond to an unlikely but possible outcome. Even though an emergency landing on water is "unlikely," as the airlines tell us, they still provide us lifejackets. And if only for peace of mind, we're glad they do. To do otherwise is a gamble few airlines would be willing to take, even though the actuarial tables are heavily weighted on their side.

Leeson strangely held two positions at Barings, ostensibly serving as both a trader and his own supervisor, but that fact is not interesting given the subject matter. That one man had such a tolerance for risk that he could create so much damage is not very interesting either. Both of those are short-term factors. Both would have ended if Leeson had either left the company or changed jobs, or if Barings had assigned a new supervisor to oversee his operations. What is more interesting is the culture at the bank that could allow these conditions to exist in the first place. Barings had lost its WHY.

The culture at Barings was no longer one in which people came to work inspired. Motivated, yes, but not inspired. Manipulated by the promise of massive payouts for performance, for sure, but not inspired to work in the best interest of the whole. As Leeson reported in his own account of how he got away with such risky behavior for so long, he said it was not that others didn't recognize that what he was doing was potentially dangerous. It was worse than that. There was a stigma against speaking out. "People at the London end of Barings," Leeson explained, "were all so know-all that nobody dared ask a stupid question in case they looked silly in front of everyone else." The lack of a clear set of values and beliefs, along with the weak culture that resulted, created the conditions for an every-man-for-himself environment, the long-term impact of which could yield little else than disaster. This is caveman stuff. If the people aren't looking out for the community, then the benefits of a community erode. Many companies have star employees and star salesmen and so on, but few have a culture that produces great people as a rule and not an exception.

Trust is a remarkable thing. Trust allows us to rely on others. We rely on those we trust for advice to help us make decisions. Trust is the bedrock for the advancement of our own lives, our families, our companies, our societies and our species. We trust those in our community to care for our children so we can go out to dinner. Given the choice between two babysitters, we're more likely to trust a babysitter with a little experience from the neighborhood than one with lots of experience from far away. We wouldn't trust someone from the outside because we don't know anything about them, we say. The reality is, we don't know anything about the local babysitter either, beyond the fact that she's from the neighborhood. In this case, we trust familiarity over experience with something quite important—the safety of our children. We trust that someone who lives in the community and more likely shares our values and beliefs is better qualified to care for the most valuable thing in our lives over someone with a long résumé but from an unfamiliar place. That's pretty remarkable. It causes some pause when we consider how we hire people: what's more important, their résumé and experience, or whether they will fit our community? Our children are probably more important than the position we want to fill at the organization, yet we seem to exercise a very different standard.

Is there a false assumption at play here as to who makes the best employee?

Historically, trust has played a bigger role in advancing companies and societies than skill set alone. Like the couple leaving their children while they go out on a date for the evening, groups from within a society would go off with confidence, knowing that their homes and families would be safe upon their return. If there were no trust, then no one would take risks. No risks would mean no exploration, no experimentation and no advancement of the society as a whole. That's a remarkable concept: only when individuals can trust the culture or organization will they take personal risks in order to advance that culture or organization as a whole. For no other reason than, in the end, it's good for their own personal health and survival.

No matter how experienced, no matter how proficient, a trapeze artist will not attempt a totally new death-defying leap without first trying it with a net below him. And depending on how death-defying the trick is, he may insist on always having a net when performing the trick. Besides its obvious advantage of catching you if you fall, the net also provides a psychological benefit. Knowing it is there gives the trapeze artist the confidence to try something he's never done before, or to do it again and again. Remove the net and he will only do the safe tricks, the ones he knows he can land. The more he trusts the quality of the net, the more he will take personal risks to make his act better. The trust the circus management gives him by providing him a net is probably afforded to other performers too. Soon all the performers will feel confident to try new things and push themselves further. That collection of personal confidence and personal risk results in the entire circus putting on a much better show. An overall better show means more customers. And the system thrives. But not without trust. For those within a community, or an organization, they must trust that their leaders provide a net—practical or emotional. With that feeling of support, those in the organization are more likely to put in extra effort that ultimately benefits the group as a whole.

I will admit that there are always those who will take the risk, for the first time or repeatedly, without the net. There will always be those who will explore regardless of who is home holding down the fort. These people sometimes earn their rightful spots as the innovators. The ones who pushed further, the ones who did things no one else would do. Some of them may advance a business or even society. And some of them end up dead before they achieve anything.

There is a big difference between jumping out of a plane with a parachute on and jumping without one. Both produce extraordinary experiences, but only one increases the likelihood of being able to try again another time. A trapeze artist with a personality predisposed to taking extraordinary risks without a net may be the star attraction in an otherwise mediocre show. But if he dies or leaves for another circus, then what? This is the paradigm in which someone is motivated by self-gain regardless of the consequences or the benefits to the organization for which he or she works. In such a case, the effort may be good for the individual and it may be good for the group, but the benefits, especially for the group, come with a time limit. Over time, this system will break down, often to the detriment of the organization. Developing trust to encourage people other than those with a predilection for risk, like Nick Leeson, is a better long-term strategy.

Great organizations become great because the people inside the organization feel protected. The strong sense of culture creates a sense of belonging and acts like a net. People come to work knowing that their bosses, colleagues and the organization as a whole will look out for them. This results in reciprocal behavior. Individual decisions, efforts and behaviors that support, benefit and protect the long-term interest of the organization as a whole.

Southwest Airlines, a company renowned for its customer focus, does not, as a matter of policy, believe the customer is always right. Southwest will not tolerate customers who abuse their staff. They would rather those customers fly on a different airline. It's a subtle irony that one of the best customer service companies in the country focuses on its employees before its customers. The trust between the management and the employees, not dogma, is what produces the great customer service. It is a prerequisite, then, for someone to trust the culture in which they work to share the values and beliefs of that culture. Without it, that employee, for example, is simply a bad fit and likely to work only for self-gain without consideration for the greater good. But if those inside the organization are a good fit, the opportunity to "go the extra mile," to explore, to invent, to innovate, to advance and, more importantly, to do so again and again and again, increases dramatically. Only with mutual trust can an organization become great.

Real Trust Comes from the Things You Can't See

"Rambo 2," said the voice over Brigadier General Jumper's radio, referring to him by his call sign. "Your group 180, twenty-five miles, closing fast."

"Barnyard radar contact," replied Rambo 2, reporting that he had picked up the enemy group on his own radar. A one-star general, John Jumper was an experienced F-15 pilot with thousands of hours of flight time and over a thousand combat hours. By all measures, he was one of the best. Born in Paris, Texas, he had enjoyed a distinguished career. He'd flown just about everything the U.S. Air Force had, from cargo planes to fighter jets. Decorated and distinguished, the commander of his own combat wing, he was the embodiment of what it meant to be a fighter pilot. Smart and confident.

But on that day, Jumper's reaction didn't match the situation he faced. By twenty-five miles, he would have been expected to fire his weapons or take some other offensive movement. Fearing that Jumper was locked onto the wrong contact on his radar, Captain Lori Robinson calmly repeated what she could see from miles away: "Rambo 2 confirm radar contact YOUR group now 190 twenty miles."

As the air weapons controller who was watching the action on her radar screen from a nearby command-and-control center, it was Lori Robinson's job to direct the pilot toward enemy aircraft so that he could use his weapons to intercept and destroy them. Unlike an air traffic controller, whose job it is to keep air traffic apart, the weapons controller has to bring the planes closer together. From the vantage point of the radar screen, only the weapons controller has the big picture, as the pilot's onboard navigation system shows only what's directly in front of the aircraft.

Captain Robinson saw her job as something bigger, however, than just staring at radar, something more profound than just being the eyes and ears for the pilots who were hurtling into harm's way at 1,500 mph. Captain Robinson knew WHY her job was important. She saw herself as responsible for clearing a path for the pilots in her care so that they could do what they needed to do, so they could push themselves and their aircraft further with greater confidence. And for this reason, she was unusually good at her job. Robinson couldn't make mistakes. If she did, she would lose the trust of her pilots, and worse, they would lose trust in themselves. You see, it's confidence that makes fighter pilots so good at their jobs.

And then it happened. Captain Robinson could tell from the calm of Jumper's voice over the radio that he was unaware of the threat coming at him. On a cloudless day, 20,000 feet over the desert, the alarm screeched in Rambo 2's $25 million, state-of-the-art fighter jet. He looked up from his radar screen and saw the enemy engaging him. "BREAK RIGHT! BREAK RIGHT!" he screamed into his radio. On October 9, 1988, Brigadier General John P. Jumper was killed.

Captain Robinson waited. There was an eerie calm. Before too long, Jumper stormed into the debriefing room at Nellis Air Force Base. "You got me killed!" he barked at Captain Robinson. Situated in the Nevada desert, Nellis is home to the Air Force Fighter Weapons School, and on that day, General John Jumper took a direct hit from a simulated missile from another U.S. Air Force jet playing the part of an enemy combatant.

"Sir, it was not my fault," Captain Robinson replied calmly. "Check the video. You'll see." General Jumper, then the 57th Wing commander, a graduate of the USAF Fighter Weapons School, and a former instructor at Nellis, routinely evaluated every detail of every training mission he flew. Pilots often relied on the video to learn from their exercises. The video didn't lie. And it didn't on that day either. It revealed that the error was indeed his, not Captain Robinson's. It was a classic blunder. He had forgotten he was part of a team. He had forgotten that what made him so good at his job was not just his ability. Jumper was one of the best because there were others who were looking out for him. A massive infrastructure of people he couldn't see.

Without question General Jumper had been given the best equipment, the best technology and the best training that money could buy. But it was the mechanics, the teachers, his fellow pilots, the culture of the Air Force and Captain Robinson who ensured that he could trust himself to get the job done. General Jumper forgot WHY he was so good and made a split-second decision that cost him his life. But this is what training is for, to learn these lessons.

Some sixteen years after his lesson over the Nevada desert, General Jumper went on to big things. Now a retired four-star general, he served as chief of staff of the U.S. Air Force from 2001 to 2005, the highest-ranking uniformed office in the entire Air Force, responsible for the organization, training and equipping of nearly 700,000 active-duty, guard, reserve and civilian forces serving in the United States and overseas. As a member of the Joint Chiefs of Staff, he, along with the other service chiefs, advised the secretary of defense, the National Security Council and the president.

This is not, however, a story about General Jumper. It is a story about Lori Robinson. Now herself a brigadier general in the Air Force, she no longer has her face down a scope. There are no more bogeys and bandits, the Air Force's nicknames for the good guys and the bad guys, in her life. Even though her job has changed,

General Robinson still starts every day by reminding herself WHY she came to work.

As much as she misses "her kids," as she called those who served under her command, General Robinson is still looking for ways she can clear a path for others so that they can push themselves and the organization further. "The time to think of yourself is done, it is not about you, it is about the lieutenants behind you," she'd remind her students when she was an instructor at the Fighter Weapons School. "If enough of us do this," she goes on, referring to WHY she does what she does, "then we leave this military and this country in better shape than we found it. And isn't that the point?" And it is that sense of purpose, a clear idea of WHY she comes to work, that has been the cornerstone of General Robinson's success. And that, incidentally, has been remarkable.

Working hard to clear a path for others so that they can confidently go on to do bigger and better things has in turn inspired others to clear a path for General Robinson to do exactly the same thing. As a woman in the very masculine world of the military, she sets an example for how to lead. Great leadership is not about flexing and intimidation; great leaders, as General Robinson proves, lead with WHY. They embody a sense of purpose that inspires those around them.

General Robinson was so trusted as a weapons controller that it was not unusual for pilots in training to request that she be assigned to them. "The greatest compliment I ever got was when people would say, 'When I go to war, I want Lori on the radio,'" she says. She is the first woman in the history of the Air Force to command the 552nd Air Control Wing out of Tinker Air Force Base, one of the largest wings in Air Combat Command (the wing that flies the AWACS airborne control aircraft—the fleet of Boeing 707s with the huge rotating radar dishes on top). She is the first commander of a combat wing ever who didn't come up through the pilot ranks. She was the first female Weapons School instructor to teach at the Air Force Fighter Weapons School, where the Air Force trains all its top guns. There, she became the most celebrated teacher in the ranks—winning best teacher seven classes in a row. She is the first female director of the Secretary of the Air Force and Chief of Staff of the Air Force Executive Action Group. In 2000, the chairman of the Joint Chiefs of Staff said of General Robinson, at the time still a captain, that she singularly influenced his ideas on airpower. And the list goes on.

By any measure, General Lori Robinson is a remarkable leader. Some in management positions operate as if they are in a tree of monkeys. They make sure that everyone at the top of the tree looking down sees only smiles. But all too often, those at the bottom looking up see only asses. Great leaders like General Robinson are respected by those both above and below. Those in her command trust her implicitly because they know she's committed to looking after them. "There's nothing you can do that I can't fix," she was often heard telling students at Fighter Weapons School. And those to whom she reports show remarkable deference to her. "I don't know how she gets away with half the stuff she does," say those who know her. More importantly, it is said with a grin and with respect. General Robinson's ability to lead developed not because she's the smartest or the nicest. She's a great leader because she understands that earning the trust of an organization doesn't come from setting out to impress everyone, it comes from setting out to serve those who serve her. It is the invisible trust that gives a leader the following they need to get things done. And in Lori Robinson's case, things get done.

I use the military because it exaggerates the point. Trust matters. Trust comes from being a part of a culture or organization with a common set of values and beliefs. Trust is maintained when the values and beliefs are actively managed. If companies do not actively work to keep their Golden Circle in balance—clarity, discipline and consistency—then trust starts to break down. A company, indeed any organization, must work actively to remind everyone WHY the company exists. WHY it was founded in the first place. What it believes. They need to hold everyone in the company accountable to the values and guiding principles. It's not enough to just write them on the wall—that's passive. Bonuses and incentives must revolve around them. The company must serve those whom they wish to serve it.

With balance, those who are good fits can trust that everyone is on board for the same reasons. It's also the only way that each individual in the system can trust that others are acting to "leave the organization in a better way than we found it," to quote General Robinson again. This is the root of passion. Passion comes from feeling like you are a part of something that you believe in, something bigger than yourself. If people do not trust that a company is organized to advance the WHY, then the passion is diluted. Without managed trust, people will show up to do their jobs and they will worry primarily about themselves. This is the root of office politics—people acting within the system for self-gain often at the expense of others, even the company. If a company doesn't manage trust, then those working for it will not trust the company, and self-interest becomes the overwhelming motivation. This may be good for the short term, but over time the organization will get weaker and weaker.

Herb Kelleher, the visionary behind Southwest Airlines, understood this better than most. He recognized that to get the best out his employees he needed to create an environment in which they felt like the company cared about them. He knew that they would naturally excel if they felt the work they did made a difference. When a journalist asked Kelleher who comes first to him, his shareholders or his employees, his response was heresy at the time (and to a large degree still is). "Well, that's easy," he said, "employees come first and if employees are treated right, they treat the outside world right, the outside world uses the company's product again, and that makes the shareholders happy. That really is the way that it works and it's not a conundrum at all."

The Influence of Others

Whom do you trust more, someone you know or someone you don't know? What do you trust more, a claim made in a piece of advertising or a recommendation from a friend? Whom do you trust more, the waiter who tells you, "Everything on the menu is great," or the waiter who tells you to avoid the chicken casserole? Are these questions too easy? Then how about this one: why should anyone trust you?

Personal recommendations go a long way. We trust the judgment of others. It's part of the fabric of strong cultures. But we don't trust the judgment of just anyone. We are more likely to trust those who share our values and beliefs. When we believe someone has our best interest in mind because it is in their benefit to do so, the whole group benefits. The advancements of societies were based a great deal on the trust between those with a common set of values and beliefs.

The feeling of trust is lodged squarely in the same place as the WHY—the limbic brain—and it's often powerful enough to trump empirical research, or at least seed doubt. This is the reason why so many manipulations are effective; we believe that, for better or worse, others know more than we do. Clearly, four out of five dentists know more than us when choosing chewing gum (but what about the one holdout . . . what did he know that the others didn't?). Of course we trust the celebrity endorsement. Those celebs are rich and can use any product they want. It must be good if they are putting their reputation on the line to promote it, right?

You probably answered that question in your head already. Clearly they are endorsing the product because they are getting paid to. But if celebrity endorsements didn't work, companies wouldn't use them. Or perhaps it's the fear that they "might" work that fuels the million-dollar wink and a smile that encourages us to choose one car over another or one lipstick over another. The fact is, none of us is immune to the effect of someone we know or *feel* like we trust influencing our decisions.

Celebrity endorsements are used with this concept in mind. By using a recognizable face or name, so the assumption goes, people will more likely trust the claims being made. The flaw in this assumption is that celebrity status alone may work to influence behavior, but at this level it's just peer pressure. For it to work, the celebrity needs to represent some clear cause or belief. An athlete known for her work ethic may have some value to a company with the same belief, for example. Or an actor known for his charitable work would be good fit for a company known for doing good. In these cases, it is clear that both the company and the celebrity are working together to advance the same cause. There used to be an ad for TD Bank that featured morning show hosts Regis Philbin and Kelly Ripa. I'm still trying to figure out the cause that two talk show hosts represent and how that matters when it comes to choosing one bank over another. When a company says that a celebrity represents "the kind of qualities we want our customers to associate with us," they miss the point. The celebrity is another WHAT to the company's WHY. The celebrity must embody the qualities that already exist at the company. Without clarity of WHY first, any benefit will amount to simply increasing recognition.

So many decisions (and indeed contract negotiations) are based on an advertising industry measurement called a Q-score—a quotient of how well recognized a celebrity is, how famous they are, so to speak. The higher the score, the better the unaided awareness of the celebrity. This information alone is not enough. The clearer the spokesperson's own WHY is understood, the better ambassador they can be for a like-minded brand or company. But there is no measurement of a celebrity's WHY currently available, so the result is obvious. The value of too many celebrity endorsements is the celebrity appeal alone. Unless the audience to which you are trying to appeal gets a sense of what that spokesperson believes, unless that spokesperson is "one of us," the enforcement may drive recognition, it may even drive sales for the short term, but it will fail to build trust.

A trusted recommendation is powerful enough to trump facts

and figures and even multimillion-dollar marketing budgets. Think of the young father who wants to do everything right for his newborn child. He decides he's going to get a new car—something safe, something to protect his child. He spends a week reading all the magazines and reports, he's seen all the advertising and decides that on Saturday he's buying a Volvo. The facts are in and his mind is made up. Friday night he and his wife head to a dinner party. Standing by the punch bowl is their friend the local car enthusiast. Our intrepid new father walks up to his friend and proudly announces that, as a new father, he's decided to buy a Volvo. Without a thought his friend replies, "Why would you do that? Mercedes is the safest car on the road. If you care about your kid, you'll get a Mercedes."

Playing on his desires to be a good father, but also trusting his friend's opinion, one of three things will happen. Our young father will either change his mind and buy a Mercedes; he will go forward with his original decision, but not without some doubt about whether he's indeed doing the right thing; or he will go back to the drawing board to redo all his research in order to reassure himself of his decision. No matter how much rational information he has at his fingertips, unless that decision also feels right, stress will go up and confidence will go down. However you slice it, the opinions of others matter. And the opinions of those we trust matter most.

The question isn't how should car companies talk to the father who bought the car. The question isn't even how they court the highly influential opinion of his friend, the car guy. The concept of buyer and influencers isn't a new one. The question is, how do you get enough of the influencers to talk about you so that you can make the system tip?

7

HOW A TIPPING POINT TIPS

If I told you I knew of a company that invented an amazing new technology that will change the way we consume TV, would that pique your interest? Perhaps you'd be interested in buying their product or investing in their company. It gets better. They have the single best product available. Their quality is through the roof, way better than anything else on the market. And their PR efforts have so been remarkable, they've even become a household name. Interested?

This is the case of TiVo. A company that seemed to have everything going for them but turned out to be a commercial and financial failure. Since they seemed to have the recipe for success, TiVo's flop defied conventional wisdom. Their struggles, however, are easily understood if you consider that they thought WHAT they did mattered more than WHY. They also ignored the Law of Diffusion of Innovations.

In 2000, Malcolm Gladwell created his own tipping point when he shared with us how tipping points happen in business and in society. In his aptly named book *The Tipping Point*, Gladwell identifies groups of necessary populations he calls connectors and influencers. With little doubt Gladwell's ideas are spot-on. But it still begs the question, why should an influencer tell anyone about you? Marketers are always trying to influence the influencers, but few really know how. We can't dispute that tipping points happen and the conditions that Gladwell articulates are right, but can a tipping point happen intentionally? They can't just be an accidental phenomenon. If they exist, then we should be able to design one, and if we can design one, we should be able to design one that lasts beyond the initial tip. It's the difference between a fad and an idea that changes an industry or society forever.

In his 1962 book *Diffusion of Innovations*, Everett M. Rogers was the first to formally describe how innovations spread through society. Thirty years later, in his book *Crossing the Chasm*, Geoffrey Moore expanded on Rogers's ideas to apply the principle to high-tech product marketing. But the Law of Diffusion of Innovations explains much more than just the spread of innovation or technology. It explains the spread of ideas.

If you don't know the law, you're likely already familiar with some of its terminology. Our population is broken into five segments that fall across a bell curve: innovators, early adoptors, early majority, late majority and laggards.

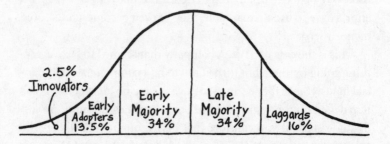

As the law states, the first 2.5 percent of the population are the innovators, and the next 13.5 percent are early adopters. Innovators, Moore says, pursue new products or ideas aggressively and are intrigued by any fundamental advance; being first is a central part of their lives. As their name suggests, innovators are the small percentage of the population that challenges the rest of us to see and think of the world a little differently.

Early adopters are similar to innovators in that they appreciate the advantages wrought by new ideas or technologies. They are early to recognize the value of new ideas and are quite willing to put up with imperfection because they can see the potential. Although quick to see the potential and willing to take risks to try new technologies or ideas, early adopters are not idea generators like the innovators. But both groups are similar, as Moore says, in that they rely heavily on their intuition. They trust their gut.

Early adopters, like innovators but to a lesser degree, are willing to pay a premium or suffer some level of inconvenience to own a product or espouse an idea that feels right. Those on the left side of the diffusion curve are the ones who stood in line for six hours to be among the first to buy the iPhone, Apple's entry into the mobile phone market, even though they could have walked into a store a week later and bought one without waiting. Their willingness to suffer an inconvenience or pay a premium had less to do with how great the product was and more to do with their own sense of who they are. They wanted to be the first.

These are also the personality types who bought flat-screen TVs when they first came out even though they cost upwards of $40,000 and the technology was still far from perfect. My friend Nathan fits this profile. I walked around his house once and counted no fewer than twelve Bluetooth earpieces for his mobile phone lying around his house. I asked him why he had so many. "Did they all break?" I queried. "No," he replied, "they came out with a new one." (There were also about five laptops, various models of BlackBerry smart phones and boxes of other gadgets lying about that never quite worked that well.) Nathan is an early adopter.

The next 34 percent of the population are the early majority, followed by the late majority, and finally the laggards on the far right side of the spectrum. Laggards are the ones who buy touchtone phones only because they don't make rotary phones anymore. The early and late majority are more practical-minded. For them, rational factors matter more. The early majority is slightly more comfortable with new ideas or technologies, while the late majority is not.

The farther right you go on the curve, the more you will encounter the clients and customers who may need what you have, but don't necessarily believe what you believe. As clients, they are the ones for whom, no matter how hard you work, it's never enough. Everything usually boils down to price with them. They are rarely loyal. They rarely give referrals and sometimes you may even wonder out loud why you still do business with them. "They just don't get it," our gut tells us. The importance of identifying this group is so that you can avoid doing business with them. Why invest good money and energy to go after people who, at the end of the day, will do business with you anyway if you meet their practical requirements but will never be loyal if you don't? It's not too hard to recognize where people fall on the spectrum once you're in a relationship with them; the opportunity is to figure out which is which before you decide to work with them.

We all sit at different places on this spectrum depending on the product or idea. Most of us are fiercely loyal to certain products and ideas at various times and demonstrate left-side-of-the-curve behavior. And for other products or ideas we exhibit right-side-of-the-curve behavior. When we sit on one side of the spectrum, we often have a hard time understanding those on the other side because their behavior doesn't make sense to us. My sister is an early adopter when it comes to fashion trends, whereas I'm firmly in the late majority. It was only recently that I finally caved and bought a pair of overpriced designer blue jeans. I admit they look good, but I still think they aren't worth the money and I can't understand why my sister thinks they are.

In contrast, I'm an early adopter for some technologies. I bought a Blu-ray DVD player before they had perfected the technology. I paid about four or five times more for it compared to a regular DVD player. My sister can't understand why I waste my money on all that "useless stuff," as she puts it. We will never see eye to eye on this stuff.

Each of us assigns different values to different things and our behaviors follow accordingly. This is one of the major reasons why it is nearly impossible to "convince" someone of the value of your products or ideas based on rational arguments and tangible benefits. It's the ol' Ferrari and Honda Odyssey debate again. Designer jean companies (or my sister) can talk to me until they are blue in the face about the importance of fabric quality, design and workmanship—it goes in one ear and out the other. Similarly, it can be proven, beyond a shadow of doubt, the rational benefits of choosing a $500 DVD player over a $100 one; my sister won't hear a word of it. And so the game of manipulation ensues. Again, although always effective, manipulations don't breed loyalty and they increase costs and stress for all parties involved.

Most people or organizations that have something to sell, be it a product, service or idea, hope to achieve some level of mass-market success or acceptance. Most hope to penetrate the bell of the curve. Getting there, however, is easier said than done. When you ask small businesses about their goals, many of them will tell you they want to be a billion-dollar business in X number of years. The odds of that happening, unfortunately, don't look good. Of the 27 million businesses registered in the United States, fewer than 2,000 ever reach a billion dollars in annual revenues. And 99.9 percent of all businesses in America have fewer than 500 employees. In other words, mass-market success is really hard to achieve.

Big companies have similar challenges repeating their mass-market success. Just because they've done it once or twice doesn't mean they know how to do it every time. The Zune, Microsoft's entry into the multigigabyte mp3 player market, for example, was pegged to "take on the iPod." It didn't happen. Even if the quality is superior, there is more to succeeding than just the product and the marketing. Don't forget, the superior Betamax technology did not beat out the substandard VHS technology as the standard format for videotape in the 1980s. The best does not always win. Like any natural law, the Law of Diffusion must be considered if mass-market acceptance is important to you. Refusal to do so will cost a lot of money and may result in a mediocre success, if not complete failure.

There is an irony to mass-market success, as it turns out. It's near impossible to achieve if you point your marketing and resources to the middle of the bell, if you attempt to woo those who represent the middle of the curve without first appealing to the early adopters. It can be done, but at massive expense. This is because the early majority, according to Rogers, will not try something until someone else has tried it first. The early majority, indeed the entire majority, need the recommendation of someone else who has already sampled the product or service. They need to know someone else has tested it. They need that trusted, personal recommendation.

According to the Law of Diffusion, mass-market success can only be achieved after you penetrate between 15 percent and 18 percent of the market. That's because the early majority won't try something new until someone else has tried it first. This is why we have to drop our price or offer value-added services. We're attempting to reduce the risk tolerance of these practical-minded people until they feel comfortable to buy. That's what a manipulation is. They may buy, but they won't be loyal. Don't forget, loyalty is when people are willing to suffer some inconvenience or pay a premium to do business with you. They may even turn down a better offer from someone else—something the late majority rarely does. The ability to get the system to tip is the point at which the growth of a business or the spreading of an idea starts to move at an extraordinary pace. It is also at this point that a product gains mass-market acceptance. The point at which an idea becomes a movement. When that happens, the growth is not only exponential, it is automatic. It just goes.

The goal of business then should not be to simply sell to anyone who wants what you have—the majority—but rather to find people who believe what you believe, the left side of the bell curve. They perceive greater value in what you do and will happily pay a premium or suffer some sort of inconvenience to be a part of your cause. They are the ones who, on their own volition, will tell others about you. That 15 to 18 percent is not made up of people who are simply willing to buy the product. It is the percentage of people who share your beliefs and want to incorporate your ideas, your products and your services into their own lives as WHATs to their own WHYs. They look to WHAT you do as a tangible element that demonstrates their own purpose, cause or belief to the outside world. Their willingness to pay a premium or suffer inconvenience to use your product or service says more about them than it does about you and your products. Their ability to easily see WHY they need to incorporate your products into their lives makes this group the most loyal customers. They are also the most loyal shareholders and the most loyal employees. No matter where they sit in the spectrum, these are the people who not only love you but talk about you. Get enough of the people on the left side of the curve on your side and they encourage the rest to follow.

I love asking businesses what their conversion is on new business efforts. Many answer proudly, "Ten percent." Even if you ignore the principles of the Golden Circle, the law of averages says you can win about 10 percent of the business. Throw enough spaghetti against the wall and some of it sticks. To grow the business, all you need to do is more prospecting, which is why growing your business by aiming at the middle of the curve is so expensive. Though the business may grow, the average will stay about the same, and 10 percent is not enough for the system to tip.

Likewise, 10 percent of your existing customers or clients will naturally show loyalty to you. But why are they so loyal? Like our inability to explain why we love our spouses, the best we can muster up to explain what makes them such great clients is, "They just get it." And though this explanation may feel right, it is completely unactionable. How do you get more people to "get it"? This is what Moore refers to as the "chasm," the transition between the early adopters and the early majority, and it's hard to cross. But not if you know WHY.

If you have the discipline to focus on the early adopters, the majority will come along eventually. But it must start with WHY. Simply focusing on so-called influencers is not enough. The challenge is, which influencers? There are those who seem to fit the influencer profile more than others, but in reality we are all influencers at different times for different reasons. You don't just want any influencer, you want someone who believes what you believe. Only then will they talk about you without any prompts or incentives. If they truly believe in what you believe and if they are truly on the left side of the curve they won't need to be incentivized; they'll do it because they want to. The entire act of incentivizing an influencer is manipulative. It renders the influencer completely inauthentic to his or her group. It won't take long for the group to find out that a recommendation wasn't made with the group's best interest in mind, but rather because of one person's self-interest. Trust erodes and the value of the influencer is rendered useless.

Refusing to Consider the Law of Diffusion Will Cost You

In 1997, TiVo was racing to market with a remarkable new device. Few would debate that from the time the product was introduced to the present day, TiVo has had the single highest-quality product in its category. The company's PR has been extraordinary. They have achieved an unaided awareness that most brands can only dream of. They have become more than generic terms, like Kleenex, Band-Aids and Q-tips. In fact, they have been able to achieve more than generic status; they are a verb in the English language, "to TiVo."

They were well funded with venture capital and had a technology that could truly reinvent how we consume television. The problem was, they marketed their technology directly to the middle of the bell curve. Seeing the mass-market appeal of the product, they ignored the principles of the Law of Diffusion and targeted the masses. Compounding that bad aim, they attempted to appeal to the cynical majority by explaining WHAT the product did instead of stating WHY the company or the product existed in the first place. They attempted to convince with features and benefits.

They basically said to the mass market:

We've got a new product.

It pauses live TV.

Skips commercials.

Rewinds live TV.

Memorizes your viewing habits and records shows on your
behalf without your needing to set it.

Analysts were intrigued by the prospects of TiVo as well as its
competitor, Replay, a well-funded start-up backed by venture capital. One market researcher estimated that these so-called personal
TV receivers would reach 760,000 subscribers by the end of the first
year.

TiVo finally shipped in 1999. Mike Ramsay and Jim Barton, two
former colleagues who had founded TiVo, were certain the TV-
viewing public was ready. And they may have been if only TiVo
knew how to talk to them. But despite the excitement among analysts and technophiles, sales were hugely disappointing. TiVo sold
about 48,000 units the first year. Meanwhile, Replay, whose back-
ers included the founders of Netscape, failed to gain a following
and instead became embroiled in a dispute with the television net-
works over the way it allowed viewers to skip ads. In 2000, the company adopted a new strategy and a few months later was sold to
SonicBlue, which later filed for bankruptcy.

Analysts were stumped as to why the TiVo machines weren't
selling better. The company seemed to have everything going for
it. After all, they had the recipe for success: a great-quality product,
money and ideal market conditions. In 2002, after TiVo had been
on the market nearly three years, a headline in *Advertising Age*
summed it up best: "More U.S. Homes Have Outhouses than
TiVos." (At the time, there were 671,000 homes with outhouses
in the United States, compared with 504,000 to 514,000 homes
with TiVo.) Not only were sales poor, but the company has not
fared well for its shareholders either. At the time of the initial public offering in the fall of 1999, TiVo stock traded at slightly over $40
per share. A few months later it hit its high at just over $50. The

stock declined steadily for the rest of the year, and except for three short periods since 2001, it has never since traded over $10.

If you apply the principles of the Golden Circle, the answer is clear—people don't buy WHAT you do, they buy WHY you do it, and TiVo attempted to convince consumers to buy by telling them only WHAT the product did. Features and rational benefits. The practical-minded, technophobic mass market's response was predictable. "I don't understand it. I don't need it. I don't like it. You're scaring me." There were a small number of TiVo loyalists, probably about 10 percent, those who just "got it," who didn't need an explicit articulation of WHY. They exist to this day, but there were not enough of them to create the tipping point that TiVo needed and predicted.

What TiVo should have done is talked about what they believed. They should have talked about WHY the product was invented in the first place, then ventured out to share their invention with the innovators and early adopters who believed what they believed. If they had started their sales pitch with WHY the product existed in the first place, the product itself would have become the proof of the higher cause—proof of WHY. If their Golden Circle was in balance, the outcome might have been quite different. Compare the original list of features and benefits with a revised version that starts with WHY:

> If you're the kind of person who likes to have total control of every aspect of your life, boy do we have a product for you.
> It pauses live TV.
> Skips commercials.
> Rewinds live TV.
> Memorizes your viewing habits and records shows on your behalf without you needing to set it.

In this version, all the features and rational benefits serve as tangible proof of WHY the product exists in the first place, not the reasons to buy, per se. The WHY is the belief that drives the decision, and WHAT it does provides us a way to rationalize the appeal of the product.

Confirming their failure to tap the right segment of the market, TiVo offered a very rational explanation of what was happening. "Until people get their hands on it," Rebecca Baer, a spokeswoman for TiVo, told the *New York Times* in 2000, "they don't understand why they need this." If this line of logic were true, then no new technology would ever take hold. A fact that is patently untrue. Though Ms. Baer was correct about the mass market's failure to understand the value, it was TiVo's failure to properly communicate and rally the left side of the bell curve to educate and encourage the adoption that was the reason so few people "got their hands on it." TiVo did not start with WHY. They ignored the left side of the curve and completely failed to find the tipping point. And for those reasons, "people didn't get their hands on it," and the mass market didn't buy it.

Fast-forward almost a decade. TiVo continues to have the best digital video-recording product on the market. Its unaided awareness continues to be through the roof. Nearly everyone knows now what the product is and what it does, yet the company's future is by no means secure.

While millions of viewers may say they "TiVo" things all the time, unfortunately for TiVo, they aren't using a TiVo system. Rather, they "TiVo" shows using a digital video recorder (DVR) provided by the cable or satellite company. Many try to make the argument that TiVo's failure was due to the cable companies' superior distribution. But we know that people often go out of their way, pay a premium or suffer an inconvenience to buy a product that resonates on a visceral level with them. Until recently, people who wanted a custom Harley-Davidson motorcycle waited upwards of six months to a year to take delivery of their product. By any standard, that's just bad service. Consumers could have just walked into a Kawasaki dealership and walked right out with a brand-new bike. They could have found a very similar model with similar power and maybe even for less money. But they suffered the inconvenience willingly, not because they were in the market for a motorcycle, but because they wanted a Harley.

TiVo is not the first to ignore these sound principles and won't be the last. The meager success of satellite radio technology like Sirius or XM Radio has followed a similar path. They offered a well-publicized, well-funded new technology that attempted to convince users with a promise of rational features and benefits—no commercials and more channels than the competition. Throw in an impressive array of celebrity endorsements, including rap star Snoop Dogg and 1970s pop icon David Bowie, and the technology still didn't stick. When you start with WHY, those who believe what you believe are drawn to you for very personal reasons. It is those who share your values and beliefs, not the quality of your products, that will cause the system to tip. Your role in the process is to be crystal clear about what purpose, cause or belief you exist to champion, and to show how your products and services help advance that cause. Absent a WHY, new ideas and technologies quickly find themselves playing the price-and-feature game—a sure sign of an absence of WHY and a slide into commodity status. It is not the technology that failed, it was how the companies tried to sell it. Satellite radio has not displaced commercial radio in any meaningful way. Even when Sirius and XM merged, hoping the joined force of their companies would help change their luck, shares for the combined company sold for less than 50 cents apiece. And, last time I checked, XM was offering a discount, a promotion, free shipping and a claim of being "America's #1 satellite radio service with over 170 channels" to push their product.

Give the People Something to Believe In

On August 28, 1963, 250,000 people from across the country descended on the Mall in Washington, D.C., to hear Dr. Martin Luther King Jr. give his famous "I Have a Dream" speech. The organizers didn't send out 250,000 invitations and there was no

Web site to check the date. How did they get a quarter of a million people to show up on the right day at the right time?

During the early 1960s, the country was torn apart by racial tensions. There were riots in dozens of cities in 1963 alone. America was a country scarred by inequality and segregation. How the civil rights movement lifted an idea that all men are created equal to become a movement with the power to change a country is grounded in the principles of The Golden Circle and the Law of Diffusion.

Dr. King was not the only person alive during that time who knew WHAT had to change to bring about civil rights in America. He had many ideas about WHAT needed to happen, but so did others. And not all of his ideas were good. He was not a perfect man; he had his complexities.

But Dr. King was absolute in his conviction. He *knew* change had to happen in America. His clarity of WHY, his sense of purpose, gave him the strength and energy to continue his fight against often seemingly insurmountable odds. There were others like him who shared his vision of America, but many of them gave up after too many defeats. Defeat is painful. And the ability to continue head-on, day after day, takes something more than knowing what legislation needs to be passed. For civil rights to truly take hold in the country, its organizers had to rally everyone. They may have been able to pass legislation, but they needed more than that, they needed to change a country. Only if they could rally a nation to join the cause, not because they had to, but because they wanted to, could any significant change endure. But no one person can effect lasting change alone. It would take others who believed what King believed.

The details of HOW to achieve civil rights or WHAT needed to be done were debatable, and different groups tried different strategies. Violence was employed by some, appeasement by others. Regardless of HOW or WHAT was being done, there was one thing everyone had in common—WHY they were doing it. It was not just Martin Luther King's unflappable conviction that was able to stir a population, but his ability to put his WHY into words. Dr. King had a gift. He talked about what he believed. And his words had the power to inspire:

> "I believe."
> "I believe."
> "I believe."

"There are two types of laws," he shared, "those that are just and those that are unjust. A just law," Dr. King expounded, "is a man-made code that squares with the moral law. An unjust law is a code that is out of harmony with the moral law. . . . Any law that uplifts the human personality is just. Any law that degrades human personality is unjust. All segregation statutes are unjust because segregation distorts the soul and damages the personality." His belief was bigger than the civil rights movement. It was about all of mankind and how we treat each other. Of course, his WHY developed as a result of the time and place in which he was born and the color of his skin, but the civil rights movement served as the ideal platform for Dr. King to bring his WHY, his belief in equality, to life.

People heard his beliefs and his words touched them deep inside. Those who believed what he believed took that cause and made it their own. And they told people what they believed. And those people told others what they believed. Some organized to get that belief out more efficiently.

And in the summer of 1963, a quarter of a million people showed up to hear Dr. King deliver his "I Have a Dream" speech on the steps of the Lincoln Memorial.

But how many people showed up for Dr. King?

Zero.

They showed up for themselves. It was what *they* believed. It was what *they* saw as an opportunity to help America become a better version of itself. It was *they* who wanted to live in a country that reflected their own values and beliefs that inspired them to get on a bus to travel for eight hours to stand in the Washington sun in the middle of August to hear Dr. King speak. Being in Washington was simply one of the things they did to prove what they believed. Showing up that day was one of the WHATs to their own WHY. This was a cause and it was their cause.

Dr. King's speech itself served as a visceral reminder of the belief shared by everyone who stood there listening. And that speech was about what he believed, not how they were going to do it. He gave the "I Have a Dream" speech, not the "I Have a Plan" speech. It was a statement of purpose and not a comprehensive twelve-point plan to achieving civil rights in America. Dr. King offered America a place to go, not a plan to follow. The plan had its place, but not on the steps of the Lincoln Memorial.

Dr. King's articulation of his belief was something powerful enough to rally those who shared that belief even if they weren't personally affected by the inequalities. Nearly a quarter of the people who came to the rally that day were white. This was a belief not about black America, this was a belief about a shared America. Dr. King was the leader of a cause. A cause for all those who believed what he believed regardless of skin color.

It wasn't the details of his plans that earned him the right to lead. It was what he believed and his ability to communicate it clearly that people followed. In essence, he, like all great leaders, became the symbol of the belief. Dr. King came to personify the cause. To this day we build statues of him to keep that belief alive and tangible. People followed him not because of his idea of a changed America. People followed him because of *their* idea of a changed America. The part of the brain that influences our behavior and decisions does not have the capacity for language. We have trouble saying clearly, in emotional terms, why we do what we do, and offer rationalizations that, though valid and true, are not powerful enough to inspire others. So when asked why they showed up that day, people pointed to Dr. King and said simply, "Because I believe."

More than anything else, what Martin Luther King Jr. gave us was clarity, a way to explain how we felt. He gave us the words that inspired us. He gave us something to believe in, something we could easily share with our friends. Everyone at the Mall that day shared a set of values and beliefs. And everyone there that day, regardless of skin color or race or sex, trusted each other. It was that trust, that common bond, that shared belief that fueled a movement that would change a nation.

We believed.
We believed.
We believed.

PART 4

HOW TO
RALLY THOSE
WHO BELIEVE

8

START WITH WHY, BUT KNOW HOW

Energy Excites. Charisma Inspires.

RAH!!!! With a roar, Steve Ballmer, the man who replaced Bill Gates as CEO of Microsoft, bursts onto the stage of the company's annual global summit meeting. Ballmer loves Microsoft—he says so in no uncertain words. He also knows how to pump up a crowd. His energy is almost folkloric. He pumps his fists and runs from one end of the stage to the other, he screams and he sweats. He is remarkable to watch and the crowd loves it. As Ballmer proves, without a doubt, energy can motivate a crowd. But can it inspire a population? What happens the next day or the next week when Ballmer's energy is not there to motivate his employees? Is energy enough to keep a company of about 80,000 people focused?

In contrast, Bill Gates is shy and awkward, a social misfit. He does not fit the stereotype of the leader of a multibillion-dollar corporation. He is not the most energetic public speaker. When Bill Gates speaks, however, people listen with bated breath. They hang on his every word. When Gates speaks, he doesn't rally a room, he inspires it. Those who hear him take what he says and carry his words with them for weeks, months or years. Gates doesn't have energy, but Bill Gates inspires.

Energy motivates but charisma inspires. Energy is easy to see, easy to measure and easy to copy. Charisma is hard to define, near impossible to measure and too elusive to copy. All great leaders have charisma because all great leaders have clarity of WHY; an undying belief in a purpose or cause bigger than themselves. It's not Bill Gates's passion for computers that inspires us, it's his undying optimism that even the most complicated problems can be solved. He believes we can find ways to remove obstacles to ensure that everyone can live and work to their greatest potential. It is his optimism to which we are drawn.

Living through the computer revolution, he saw the computer as a perfect technology to help us all become more productive and achieve our greatest potential. That belief inspired his vision of a PC on every desk to come to life. Ironic considering Microsoft never even made PCs. It wasn't just WHAT computers did that Gates saw the impact for the new technology, it was WHY we needed them. Today, the work he does with the Bill and Melinda Gates Foundation has nothing to do with software, but it is another way he has found to bring his WHY to life. He is looking for ways to solve problems. He still has an undying belief. And he still believes that if we can help people, this time those with less privilege, remove some seemingly simple obstacles, then they too will have an opportunity to be more productive and lift themselves up to achieve their great potential. For Gates, all that has changed is WHAT he is doing to bring his cause to life.

Charisma has nothing to do with energy; it comes from a clarity of WHY. It comes from absolute conviction in an ideal bigger than oneself. Energy, in contrast, comes from a good night's sleep or lots of caffeine. Energy can excite. But only charisma can inspire. Charisma commands loyalty. Energy does not.

Energy can always be injected into an organization to motivate people to do things. Bonuses, promotions, other carrots and even a few sticks can get people to work harder, for sure, but the gains are, like all manipulations, short-term. Over time, such tactics cost more money and increase stress for employee and employer alike, and eventually will become the main reason people show up for work every day. That's not loyalty. That's the employee version of repeat business. Loyalty among employees is when they turn down more money or benefits to continue working at the same company. Loyalty to a company trumps pay and benefits. And unless you're an astronaut, it's not the work we do that inspires us either. It's the cause we come to work for. We don't want to come to work to build a wall, we want to come to work to build a cathedral.

The Chosen Path

Raised in Ohio, sixty miles from Dayton, Neil Armstrong grew up on a healthy diet of stories about the Wright brothers. From a very early age he dreamed of flying. He'd make model airplanes, read magazines about flying and stare at the heavens through a telescope mounted on the roof of his house. He even got his pilot's license before he got his driver's license. With a childhood passion that became reality, Armstrong was destined to become an astronaut. For the rest of us, however, our careers paths are more like Jeff Sumpter's.

While Sumpter was in high school, his mother arranged for him to get a summer internship at the bank where she worked. Four years after he finished high school he called the bank to see if he could do some part-time work, and they eventually offered him a full-time job. Whamo, Jeff's got a career as a banker. In fact, after fifteen years in the industry he and a colleague by the name of Trey Maust went on to start their own bank, Lewis & Clark Bank in Portland, Oregon.

Sumpter is very good at what he does—he's been one of the top-performing loan officers throughout his career. He's well liked and well respected among his colleagues and clients. But even Jeff will admit that he doesn't have much of a passion for banking, per se. Though he's not living out his childhood dream, he is passionate for something. It's not WHAT he does that gets him out of bed every morning. It's WHY he does it.

Our career paths are largely incidental. I never planned to be doing what I'm doing now. As a kid I wanted to be an aeronautical engineer, but in college I set my sights on becoming a criminal prosecutor. While I was in law school, however, I became disillusioned with the idea of being a lawyer. It just didn't feel right. I was at law school in England, where the law is one of the last truly "English" professions; not wearing a pin-striped suit to an interview could hurt my chances of getting a job. This was not my cup of tea.

I happened to be dating a young woman who was studying marketing at Syracuse University. She could see what inspired me and what frustrated me about the law and suggested I try my hand in the field. And whamo, I'd gotten myself a new career in marketing. But that's just one of the things I've done—it's not my passion and it's not how I define my life. My cause—to inspire people to do the things that inspire them—is WHY I get out of bed every day. The excitement is trying to find new ways, different WHATs to bring my cause to life, of which this book is one.

Regardless of WHAT we do in our lives, our WHY—our driving purpose, cause or belief—never changes. If our Golden Circle is in balance, WHAT we do is simply the tangible way we find to breathe life into that cause. Developing software was merely one of the things Bill Gates did to bring his cause to life. An airline gave Herb Kelleher the perfect outlet to spread his belief in freedom. Putting a man on the moon was one goal John F. Kennedy used to rally people to bring to life his belief that service to the nation—and not being serviced by the nation—would lead America to advance and prosper. Apple gave Steve Jobs a way to challenge the status quo and do something big in the world. All the things these charismatic leaders did were the tangible ways they found to bring their WHYs to life. But none of them could have imagined WHAT they would be doing when they were young.

When a WHY is clear, those who share that belief will be drawn to it and maybe want to take part in bringing it to life. If that belief is amplified it can have the power to rally even more believers to raise their hands and declare, "I want to help." With a group of believers all rallying around a common purpose, cause or belief, amazing things can happen. But it takes more than inspiration to become great. Inspiration only starts the process; you need something more to drive a movement.

Amplify the Source of Inspiration

The Golden Circle is not just a communication tool; it also provides some insight into how great organizations are organized. As we start to add dimension to the concept of the Golden Circle, it is no longer helpful to look at it as a purely two-dimensional model. If it is to provide any real value in how to build a great organization in our very three-dimensional world, the Golden Circle needs to be three-dimensional. The good news is, it is. It is, in fact, a top-down view of a cone. Turn it on its side and you can see its full value.

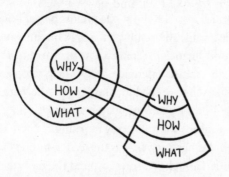

The cone represents a company or an organization—an inherently hierarchical and organized system. Sitting at the top of the system, representing the WHY, is a leader; in the case of a company, that's usually the CEO (or at least we hope it is). The next level down, the HOW level, typically includes the senior executives who are inspired by the leader's vision and know HOW to bring it to life. Don't forget that a WHY is just a belief, HOWs are the actions we take to realize that belief and WHATs are the results of those actions. No matter how charismatic or inspiring the leader is, if there are not people in the organization inspired to bring that vision to reality, to build an infrastructure with systems and processes, then at best, inefficiency reigns, and at worst, failure results.

In this rendering the HOW level represents a person or a small group responsible for building the infrastructure that can make a WHY tangible. That may happen in marketing, operations, finance, human resources and all the other C-suite departments. Beneath that, at the WHAT level, is where the rubber meets the road. It is at this level that the majority of the employees sit and where all the tangible stuff actually happens.

I Have a Dream (and He's Got the Plan)

Dr. King said he had a dream, and he inspired people to make his dream their own. What Ralph Abernathy lent the movement was something else: he knew what it would take to realize that dream, and he showed people HOW to do it. He gave the dream structure. Dr. King spoke about the philosophical implications of the movement, while Abernathy, Dr. King's onetime mentor, long-time friend and financial secretary and treasurer of the Southern Christian Leadership Conference, would help people understand the specific steps they needed to take. "Now," Abernathy would tell the audience following a rousing address by Dr. King, "let me tell you what that means for tomorrow morning."

Dr. Martin Luther King Jr. was the leader, but he didn't change America alone. Though Dr. King inspired the movement, to actually move people requires organizing. As is the case with almost all great leaders, there were others around Dr. King who knew better HOW to do that. For every great leader, for every WHY-type, there is an inspired HOW-type or group of HOW-types who take the intangible cause and build the infrastructure that can give it life. That infrastructure is what actually makes any measurable change or success possible.

The leader sits at the top of the cone—at the start, the point of WHY—while the HOW-types sit below and are responsible for actually making things happen. The leader imagines the destination and the HOW-types find the route to get there. A destination without a route leads to meandering and inefficiency, something a great many WHY-types will experience without the help of others to ground them. A route without a destination, however, may be efficient, but to what end? It's all fine and good to know how to drive, but it's more fulfilling when you have a place to go. For Dr. King, Ralph Abernathy was one of those he inspired and who knew HOW to make the cause actionable and tangible. "Dr. King's job was to interpret the ideology and theology of non-violence," said Abernathy. "My job was more simple and down-to-earth. I would tell [people], 'Don't ride those buses.'"

In every case of a great charismatic leader who ever achieved anything of significance, there was always a person or small group lurking in the shadows who knew HOW to take the vision and make it a reality. Dr. King had a dream. But no matter how inspiring a dream may be, a dream that cannot come to life stays a dream. Dr. King dreamed of many of the same things as countless other African Americans who grew up in the pre–civil rights South. He spoke of many of the same themes. He felt the same outrage perpetrated by an unjust system. But it was King's unflappable optimism and his words that inspired a population.

Dr. King didn't change America by himself. He wasn't a legislator, for example, but legislation was created to give all people in the United States equal rights regardless of skin color. It wasn't Dr. King who changed America; it was the movement of millions of others whom he inspired that changed the course of history. But how do you organize millions of people? Forget millions, how do you organize hundreds or tens of people? The vision and charisma of the leader are enough to attract the innovators and the early adopters. Trusting their guts and their intuition, these people will make the greatest sacrifices to help see the vision become a reality. With each success, with every tangible demonstration that the vision can in fact become reality, the more practical-minded majority starts to take interest. What was previously just a dream soon becomes a provable and tangible reality. And when that happens, a tipping point can be reached and then things really get moving.

Those Who Know WHY Need Those Who Know HOW

The pessimists are usually right, to paraphrase Thomas Friedman, author of *The World Is Flat*, but it's the optimists who change the world. Bill Gates imagined a world in which the computer could help us all reach our greatest potential. And it happened. Now he imagines a world in which malaria does not exist. And it will happen. The Wright brothers imagined a world in which we'd all take to the skies as easily as we catch the bus. And it happened. WHY-types have the power to change the course of industries or even the world . . . if only they knew HOW.

WHY-types are the visionaries, the ones with the overactive imaginations. They tend to be optimists who believe that all the things they imagine can actually be accomplished. HOW-types live more in the here and now. They are the realists and have a clearer sense of all things practical. WHY-types are focused on the things most people can't see, like the future. HOW-types are focused on things most people can see and tend to be better at building structures and processes and getting things done. One is not better than the other, they are just different ways people naturally see and experience the world. Gates is a WHY-type. So were the Wright brothers. And Steve Jobs. And Herb Kelleher. But they didn't do it alone. They couldn't. They needed those who knew HOW.

"If it hadn't been for my big brother, I'd have been in jail several times for checks bouncing," said Walt Disney, only half joking, to a Los Angeles audience in 1957. "I never knew what was in the bank. He kept me on the straight and narrow." Walt Disney was a WHY-type, a dreamer whose dream came true thanks to the help of his more sensible older brother Roy, a HOW-type.

Walt Disney began his career creating cartoon drawings for advertisements, but moved quickly to making animated movies. It was 1923 and Hollywood was emerging as the heart of the movie business, and Walt wanted to be part of it. Roy, who was eight years older, had been working at a bank. Roy was always in awe of his brother's talent and imagination, but he also knew that Walt was prone to taking risks and to neglecting business affairs. Like all WHY guys, Walt was busy thinking about what the future looked like and often forgot he was living in the present. "Walt Disney dreamed, drew and imagined, Roy stayed in the shadow, forming an empire," wrote Bob Thomas, a Disney biographer. "A brilliant financier and businessman, Roy helped turn Walt Disney's dreams into reality, building the company that bears his brother's name." It was Roy who founded the Buena Vista Distribution Company that made Disney films a central part of American childhood. It was Roy who created the merchandising business that transformed Disney characters into household names. And, like almost every HOW-type, Roy never wanted to be the front man; he preferred to stay in the background and focus on HOW to build his brother's vision.

Most people in the world are HOW-types. Most people are quite functional in the real world and can do their jobs and do very well. Some may be very successful and even make millions of dollars, but they will never build billion-dollar businesses or change the world. HOW-types don't need WHY-types to do well. But WHY-guys, for all their vision and imagination, often get the short end of the stick. Without someone inspired by their vision and the knowledge to make it a reality, most WHY-types end up as starving visionaries, people with all the answers but never accomplishing much themselves.

Although so many of them fancy themselves visionaries, in reality most successful entrepreneurs are HOW-types. Ask an entrepreneur what they love about being an entrepreneur and most will tell you they love to build things. That they talk about building is a sure clue that they know HOW to get things done. A business is a structure—systems and processes that need to be assembled. It is the HOW-types who are more adept at building those processes and systems. But most companies, no matter how well built, do not become billion-dollar businesses or change the course of industries. To reach the billion-dollar status, to alter the course of an industry, requires a very special and rare partnership between one who knows WHY and those who know HOW.

In nearly every case of a person or an organization that has gone on to inspire people and do great things, there exists this special partnership between WHY and HOW. Bill Gates, for example, may have been the visionary who imagined a world with a PC on every desk, but Paul Allen built the company. Herb Kelleher was able to personify and preach the cause of freedom, but it was Rollin King who came up with the idea for Southwest Airlines. Steve Jobs was the rebel's evangelist, but Steve Wozniak is the engineer who made the Apple work. Jobs had the vision, Woz had the goods. It is the partnership of a vision of the future and the talent to get it done that makes an organization great.

This relationship starts to clarify the difference between a vision statement and a mission statement in an organization. The vision is the public statement of the founder's intent, WHY the company exists. It is literally the vision of a future that does not yet exist. The mission statement is a description of the route, the guiding principles—HOW the company intends to create that future. When both of those things are stated clearly, the WHY-type and the HOW-type are both certain about their roles in the partnership. Both are working together with clarity of purpose and a plan to get there. For it to work, however, it requires more than a set of skills, it requires trust.

As discussed at length in part 3, trusting relationships are invaluable for us to feel safe. Our ability to trust people or organizations allows us to take risks and feel supported in our efforts. And perhaps the most trusting relationship that exists is between the visionary and the builder, the WHY-guy and the HOW-guy. In organizations able to inspire, the best chief executives are WHY-types—people who wake up every day to lead a cause and not just run a company. In these organizations, the best chief financial officers and chief operating officers are high-performing HOW-types, those with the strength of ego to admit they are not visionaries themselves but are inspired by the leader's vision and know how to build the structure that can bring it to life. The best HOW-types generally do not want to be out front preaching the vision; they prefer to work behind the scenes to build the systems that can make the vision a reality. It takes the combined skill and effort of both for great things to happen.

It's not an accident that these unions of WHY and HOW so often come from families or old friendships. A shared upbringing and life experience increases the probability of a shared set of values and beliefs. In the case of family or childhood friends, upbringing and common experiences are nearly exactly the same. That's not to say you can't find a good partner somewhere else. It's just that growing up with somebody and having a common life experience increases the likelihood of a shared common worldview.

Walt Disney and Roy Disney were brothers. Bill Gates and Paul Allen went to high school together in Seattle. Herb Kelleher was Rollin King's divorce attorney and old friend. Martin Luther King Jr. and Ralph Abernathy both preached in Birmingham, long before the civil rights movement took form. And Steve Jobs and Steve Wozniak were best friends in high school. The list goes on.

To Run or To Lead

For all the talented HOW-types running today's organizations, they can achieve success that will last their lifetimes, but they will spend their lifetimes running their companies. There are many ways to be successful and drive profits. Any number of manipulations, only some of which I've touched upon in this book, work quite well. Even the ability to create a tipping point is possible without creating lasting change. It's called a fad. But great organizations function exactly like any social movement. They inspire people to talk about a product or idea, include that product in the context of their lifestyle, share the idea or even find ways to advance the prosperity of the organization itself. Great organizations not only excite the human spirit, they inspire people to take part in helping to advance the cause without needing to pay them or incentivize them in any particular way. No cash-back incentives or mail-in rebates required. People feel compelled to spread the word, not because they have to, but because they want to. They willingly take up arms to share the message that inspires them.

Build a Megaphone That Works

After a three-month selection process, BCI finally chose a new ad agency to help develop a campaign to launch their new product line. Big Company Incorporated is a well-known brand operating in a fairly cluttered market space. As a manufacturer, their products are sold via a third-party sales force, often on the shelves of big-box retailers, so they don't have direct control over the sales process. The best they can do is to try to influence the sale from a distance—with marketing. BCI is a good company with a strong culture. The employees respect the management, and in general the company does good work. But over the years the competition has grown fairly stiff. And although BCI has a good product and competitive pricing, it is still tough to maintain strong growth year over year. This year, BCI management is particularly excited because the company is launching a new product they really think will make BCI stand out. To help promote it, BCI's agency has launched a major new ad campaign.

"From the leading maker," says the new ad, "comes the newest, most innovative product you've ever seen." The ad goes on to talk about all the new features and benefits, and includes something about the "quality you've come to expect from BCI," something the BCI executives felt quite strongly about including. BCI executives have worked hard to build their company's reputation and they want to leverage it. They are very excited about their new campaign and are really banking on the success of this product to help drive sales in general. They know they do good work, and they want to get the message out. They need it to be loud. And with a budget of millions of dollars to advertise their new product, in that respect, BCI succeeds.

But there is a problem.

BCI and their agency did a good job of telling people about their new product. The work was quite creative. They were able to explain what was new and special about their latest innovation, and focus groups agreed that the new product was much better than that of the competition. The millions of dollars in media ensured that lots of people would see their advertising and see it often. Their reach and frequency, the measurement commonly used by ad agencies to gauge the number of people exposed to the advertising, was very good. There is no doubt that their message was loud. The problem was, it wasn't clear. It was all WHATs and HOW and no WHY. Even though people learned what the product did, no one knew what BCI believed. The good news is, it's not a complete loss; the products will sell as long as the ads are on the air and the promotions remain competitive. It's an effective strategy, but an expensive way to make money.

What if Martin Luther King had delivered a comprehensive twelve-point plan about achieving civil rights in America, a plan more comprehensive than any other plan for civil rights ever offered? Booming through the speakers that summer's day in 1963, his message would have been loud. Microphones, like advertising and PR, are fantastic for making sure a message is heard. Like BCI, King's message would still have reached thousands of people. But his belief would not have been clear.

Volume is reasonably easy to achieve. All it takes is money or stunts. Money can pay to keep a message front and center. And publicity stunts are good at getting on the news. But neither plants seeds of loyalty. Many reading this may remember that Oprah Winfrey once gave away a free car to every member of her studio audience. It happened several years ago, in 2004, and still people refer to the stunt. But how many can recall the model of car she gave away? That's the problem. It was Pontiac that donated $7 million worth of cars, 276 of their new G6 model, to be exact. And it was Pontiac that saw the stunt as a way to market their new car. Yet although the stunt worked well to reinforce Oprah's generous nature, something with which we are all familiar, few remember that Pontiac was a part of the event. Worse, the stunt didn't do anything to reinforce some purpose, cause or belief that Pontiac represents. We had no idea what Pontiac's WHY was before the stunt, so it's hard for the publicity stunt to do much more than, well, be a stunt to get some publicity. With no sense of WHY, there is nothing else it's doing.

For a message to have real impact, to affect behavior and seed loyalty, it needs more than publicity. It needs to publicize some higher purpose, cause or belief to which those with similar values and beliefs can relate. Only then can the message create any lasting mass-market success. For a stunt to appeal to the left side of the curve of the Law of Diffusion, WHY the stunt is being performed, beyond the desire to generate press, must be clear. Though there may be short-term benefits without clarity, loud is nothing more than excessive volume. Or in business vernacular: clutter. And companies wonder why differentiation is such a challenge these days. Have you heard the volume coming from some of them?

In contrast, what would have been the impact of Dr. King's speech had he not had a microphone and loudspeakers? His vision would have been no less clear. His words would have been no less inspiring. He knew what he believed and he spoke with passion and charisma about that belief. But only the few people with front-row seats would have been inspired by those words. A leader with a cause, whether it be an individual or an organization, must have a megaphone through which to deliver his message. And it must be clear and loud to work. Clarity of purpose, cause or belief is important, but it is equally important that people hear you. For a WHY to have the power to move people it must not only be clear, it must be amplified to reach enough people to tip the scale.

It's no coincidence that the three-dimensional Golden Circle is a cone. It is, in practice, a megaphone. An organization effectively becomes the vessel through which a person with a clear purpose, cause or belief can speak to the outside world. But for a megaphone to work, clarity must come first. Without a clear message, what will you amplify?

Say It Only If You Believe It

Dr. King used his megaphone to rally throngs of people to follow him in pursuit of social justice. The Wright brothers used their megaphone to rally their local community to help them build the technology that could change the world. Thousands of people heard John F. Kennedy's belief in service and rallied to put a man on the moon in less than a decade. The ability to excite and inspire people to go out of their way to contribute to something bigger than themselves is not unique to social causes. Any organization is capable of building a megaphone that can achieve a huge impact. In fact, it is one of the defining factors that makes an organization great. Great organizations don't just drive profits, they lead people, and they change the course of industries and sometimes our lives in the process.

A clear sense of WHY sets expectations. When we don't know an organization's WHY, we don't know what to expect, so we expect the minimum—price, quality, service, features—the commodity stuff. But when we do have a sense for the WHY, we expect more. For those not comfortable being held to a higher standard, I strongly advise against trying to learn your WHY or keeping your Golden Circle in balance. Higher standards are hard to maintain. It requires the discipline to constantly talk about and remind everyone WHY the organization exists in the first place. It requires that everyone in the organization be held accountable to HOW you do things—to your values and guiding principles. And it takes time and effort to ensure that everything you say and do is consistent with your WHY. But for those willing to put in the effort, there are some great advantages.

Richard Branson first built Virgin Records into a multibillion-dollar retail music brand. Then he started a successful record label.

Later he started an airline that is today considered one of the premier airlines in the world. He then started a soda brand, wedding-planning company, insurance company and mobile phone service. And the list goes on. Likewise, Apple sells us computers, mobile phones, DVRs and mp3 players, and has replicated their capacity for innovation again and again. The ability of some companies not to just succeed but to repeat their success is due to the loyal followings they command, the throngs of people who root for their success. In the business world, they say Apple is a lifestyle brand. They underestimate Apple's power. Gucci is a lifestyle brand—Apple changes the course of industries. By any definition these few companies don't function like corporate entities. They exist as social movements.

Repeating Greatness

Ron Bruder is not a household name, but he is a great leader. In 1985, he stood at a crosswalk with his two daughters waiting for the light to change so they could cross the street. A perfect opportunity, he thought, to teach the young girls a valuable life lesson. He pointed across the street to the red glow of the "Do Not Walk" signal and asked them what they thought that sign meant. "It means we have to stand here," they replied. "Are you sure?" he asked rhetorically. "How do you know it's not telling us to run?"

Soft-spoken and almost always wearing a well-tailored three-piece suit when he comes to work, Bruder looks like you would imagine a conservative executive to look like. But don't assume you know how things work simply based on what you see. Bruder is anything but a stereotype. Though he has enjoyed the trappings of success, he is not motivated by them. They have always been the unintended by-product of his work. Bruder is driven by a clear sense of WHY. He sees a world in which people accept the lives they live and do the things they do not because they have to, but because no one ever showed them an alternative. This is the lesson he was teaching his daughters that day at the crosswalk—there is always another perspective to be considered. That Bruder always starts with WHY has enabled him to achieve great things for himself. But more significantly, it is his ability to share his WHY through the things he does that inspires those around him to do great things for themselves.

Like most of us, the career path Bruder has followed is incidental. But WHY he does things has never changed. Everything Bruder has ever done starts with his WHY, his unyielding belief that if you can simply show someone that an alternative route is possible, it can open the possibility that such a route can be followed. Though the work he is doing today is world-altering, Bruder hasn't always been in the world peace business. Like many inspiring leaders, he has changed the course of an industry. But Ron Bruder is no one-hit wonder. He has been able to repeat his success and change the course of multiple industries, multiple times.

A senior executive at a large food conglomerate that sold vegetables, canned goods and meats decided to buy a travel agency for his nephew. He asked Bruder, as the chief financial officer of the company at the time, to take a look at the financials of the agency before he went through with the purchase. Seeing an opportunity others didn't, Bruder decided to join the small travel agency to help lead it. Once there, he saw how all the other travel agencies worked and took an alternative course. Greenwell became the first travel agency on the eastern seaboard to take advantage of new technologies and fully computerize their operations. Not only did they become one of the most successful companies in the region, but after only a year, their business model became a standard for the whole industry. Then Bruder did it again.

A former client of Bruder's, Sam Rosengarten, was in some dirty businesses—coal, oil and gas; all industries that created brownfields, land that had been contaminated by their operations. Little could be done with brownfields. They were too polluted to develop, and the liability to clean them up was so high that the insurance premiums alone made it too prohibitive to even try. But Bruder doesn't see challenges the same way as everyone else. Most avoided brownfields because they could only see the cost to clean them up. Bruder focused instead on the actual cleaning. His alternative perspective revealed the perfect solution.

Bruder had already formed his real estate development company, Brookhill, and with eighteen employees, he was doing quite well. Knowing what he needed to do to seize the opportunity, he approached Dames & Moore, one of the largest environmental engineering companies in the world, and shared his new perspective with them. They loved his idea and formed a partnership to pursue it. With an engineering company with 18,000 people on board, the perceived risk was greatly minimized and the insurance companies were happy to offer affordable insurance. With affordable insurance in place, Credit Suisse First Boston offered financing that gave Brookhill the ability to buy, remediate, redevelop and sell almost $200 million worth of former environmentally contaminated properties. Brookhill, so called because Bruder comes from Brooklyn and, as he puts it, "it's a long, uphill climb to get out of Brooklyn," was the pioneer of the brownfield redevelopment industry. An industry that thrives to this day. Bruder's WHY not only steered a path that was good for business, but in the process also helped clean up the environment.

It doesn't matter WHAT Ron Bruder does. The industries and the challenges are incidental. What never changes is WHY he does things. Bruder knows that, no matter how good an opportunity looks on paper, no matter how smart he is and no matter his track record, he would never be able to achieve anything unless there were others to help him. He knows that success is a team sport. He has a remarkable ability to attract those who believe what he believes. Talented people are drawn to him with one request: "How can I help?" Having defied accepted perspectives and revolutionized more than one industry, Bruder has now set his sights on a bigger challenge: world peace. He founded the Education for Employment Foundation, the megaphone that would help him do it.

The EFE Foundation is making significant headway in helping young men and women in the Middle East to significantly alter the course of their lives and indeed the course of the region. Just has he taught his daughters at the crosswalk that there is always an alternative route, he brings an alternative perspective to the problems in Middle East. Like all Bruder's past successes, the EFE Foundation will drive businesses and do tremendous amounts of good in the process. Bruder doesn't run companies, he leads movements.

All Movements Are Personal

It started on September 11, 2001. Like so many of us, Bruder turned his attention to the Middle East after the attacks to ask why something like that could happen. He understood that if such an event could happen once, it could happen again, and for the lives of his own daughters he wanted to find a way to prevent that.

In the course of trying to figure out what he could do, he made a remarkable discovery that went much deeper than protecting his daughters or even the prevention of terrorism in the United States. In America, he realized, the vast majority of young people wake up in the morning with a feeling that there is opportunity for them in the future. Regardless of the economy, most young boys and girls who grow up in the United States have an inherent sense of optimism that they can achieve something if they want to—to live the American Dream. A young boy growing up in Gaza or a young girl living in Yemen does not wake up every day with the same feeling. Even if they have the desire, the same optimism is not there. It is too easy to point and say that the culture is different. That is not actionable. The real reason is that there is a distinct lack of institutions to give young people in the region a sense of optimism for their future. A college education in Jordan, for example, may offer some social status, but it doesn't necessarily prepare a young adult for what lies ahead. The education system, in cases like this, perpetuates a systemic cultural pessimism.

Bruder realized the problems we face with terrorism in the West have less to do with what young boys and girls in the Middle East think about America and more to do with what they think about themselves and their own vision of the future. Through the EFE Foundation, Bruder is setting up programs across the Middle East to teach young adults the hard and soft skills that will help them feel like they have opportunity in life. To feel like they can be in control of their own destinies. Bruder is using the EFE Foundation to share his WHY on a global scale—to teach people that there is always an alternative to the path they think they are on.

The Education for Employment Foundation is not an American charity hoping to do good in faraway lands. It is a global movement. Each EFE operation runs independently, with locals making up the majority of their local boards. Local leaders take personal responsibility to give young men and women that feeling of opportunity by giving them the skills, knowledge and, most importantly, the confidence to choose an alternative path for themselves. Mayyada Abu-Jaber is leading the movement in Jordan. Mohammad Naja is spreading the cause in Gaza and the West Bank. And Maeen Aleryani is proving that a cause can even change a culture in Yemen.

In Yemen, children can expect to receive nine years of education. This is one of the lowest rates in the world. In the United States, children can expect sixteen years. Inspired by Bruder, Aleryani sees such an amazing opportunity for young men and women to change their perspective and take greater control of their own future. He set out to find money to jump-start his EFE operation in Sana'a, Yemen's capital, and in one week was able to raise $50,000. The speed at which he raised that amount is pretty good even by our philanthropic standards. But this is Yemen, and Yemen has no culture of philanthropy, making his achievement that much more remarkable. Yemen is also one of the poorest nations in the region. But when you tell people WHY you're doing what you're doing, remarkable things happen.

Across the region, everyone involved in EFE believes that they can help teach their brothers and sisters and sons and daughters the skills that will help them change the path that they *think* they are on. They are working to help the youth across the region believe that their future is bright and full of opportunity. And they don't do it for Bruder, they do it for themselves. That's the reason EFE will change the world.

Sitting at the top of the megaphone, at the point of WHY, Bruder's role is to inspire, to start the movement. But it is those who believe who will effect the real change and keep the movement going. Anyone, regardless of where they live, what they do, or their nationality, can participate in this movement. It's about feeling like we belong. If you believe that there is an alternative path to the one we're on, and all we have to do is point to it, then visit the Web site efefoundation.org and join the movement. To change the world takes the support of all those who believe.

9

KNOW WHY. KNOW HOW. THEN WHAT?

They marched in, single file. Not a word was spoken. No one made any eye contact with anyone else. They all looked the same. Their heads shaved, their clothes gray and tattered. Their boots dusty. One by one, they filled a large, cavernous room, like a hangar from a science fiction movie. The only color was gray. The walls were gray. Dust and smoke filled the space making even the air look gray.

Hundreds, maybe even thousands of these drone-people sat on neatly organized benches. Row after row after row. A sea of gray conformity. They all watched a projection of a huge talking head on the screen in the front of the room that filled the entire wall. This apparent leader recited dogma and propaganda, stating proudly that they were in complete control. They had achieved perfection. They were free of pests. Or so they thought.

Running down one of the tunnels that led into the cavernous hangar, a lone blonde woman. She wore bright red shorts and a crisp white T-shirt. Like a lighthouse, her complexion and the color of her clothes seemed to shine through gray air. Pursued by security, she ran with a sledgehammer. This would not end well for the status quo.

On January 22, 1984, Apple launched their Macintosh computer with their now-famous commercial depicting an Orwellian scene of a totalitarian regime holding control over a population and promised that "1984 won't be like *1984*." But this advertising was much more than just advertising. It was not about the features and benefits of a new product. It was not about a "differentiating value proposition." It was, for all intents and purposes, a manifesto. A poetic ode to Apple's WHY, it was the film version of an individual rebelling against the status quo, igniting a revolution. And though their products have changed and fashions have changed, this commercial is as relevant today as it was twenty-five years ago when it first aired. And that's because a WHY never changes. WHAT you do can change with the times, but WHY you do it never does.

The commercial is one of the many things the company has done or said over the years to show or tell the outside world what they believe. All Apple's advertising and communications, their products, partnerships, their packaging, their store design, they are all WHATs to Apple's WHY, proof that they actively challenge status quo thinking to empower the individual. Ever notice that their advertising never shows groups enjoying their products? Always individuals. Their Think Different campaign depicted individuals who thought differently, never groups. Always individuals. And when Apple tells us to "Think Different," they are not just describing themselves. The ads showed pictures of Pablo Picasso, Martha Graham, Jim Henson, Alfred Hitchcock, to name a few, with the line "Think Different" on the upper right hand side of the page. Apple does not embody the rebel spirit because they associated themselves with known rebels. They chose known rebels because they embody the same rebel spirit. The WHY came before the creative solution in the advertising. Not a single ad showed a group. This is no accident. Empowering the individual spirit is WHY Apple exists. Apple knows their WHY and so do we. Agree with them or not, we know what they believe because they tell us.

Speak Clearly and Ye Shall Be Clearly Understood

An organization is represented by the cone in the three-dimensional view of The Golden Circle. This organized system sits atop another

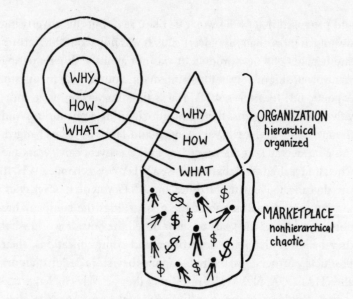

system: the marketplace. The marketplace is made up of all the customers and potential customers, all the press, the shareholders, all the competition, suppliers and all the money. This system is inherently chaotic and disorganized. The only contact that the organized system has with the disorganized system is at the base—at the WHAT level. Everything an organization says and does communicates the leader's vision to the outside world. All the products and services that the company sells, all the marketing and advertising, all the contact with the world outside communicate this. If people don't buy WHAT you do, they buy WHY you do it, and if all the things happening at the WHAT level do not clearly represent WHY the company exists, then the ability to inspire is severely complicated.

When a company is small, this is not an issue because the founder has plenty of direct contact with the outside world. Trusted HOW-types may be in short supply and the founder opts to make a majority of the big decisions. The founder or leader actually goes out and talks to customers, sells the product and hires most if not all the employees. As the company grows, however, systems and processes are added and other people will join. The cause embodied by an individual slowly morphs into a structured organization and the cone starts to take shape. As it grows, the leader's role changes. He will no longer be the loudest part of the megaphone; he will become the source of the message that is to flow through the megaphone.

When a company is small, it revolves around the personality of the founder. There is no debate that the founder's personality is the personality of the company. Why then do we think things change just because a company is successful? What's the difference between Steve Jobs the man and Apple the company? Nothing. What's the difference between Sir Richard Branson's personality and Virgin's personality? Nothing. As a company grows, the CEO's job is to personify the WHY. To ooze of it. To talk about it. To preach it. To be a symbol of what the company believes. They are the intention and WHAT the company says and does is their voice. Like Martin Luther King and his social movement, the leader's job is no longer to close all the deals; it is to inspire.

As the organization grows, the leader becomes physically removed, further and further away from WHAT the company does, and even farther away from the outside market. I love asking CEOs what their biggest priority is, and depending on their size or structure, I generally get one of two answers: customers or shareholders. Sadly, there aren't many CEOs of companies of any reasonable size who have daily contact with customers anymore. And customers and shareholders alike both exist outside the organization in the chaotic world of the marketplace. Just as the cone demonstrates, the CEO's job, the leader's responsibility, is not to focus on the outside market—it's to focus on the layer directly beneath: HOW. The leader must ensure that there are people on the team who believe what they believe and know HOW to build it. The HOW-types are responsible for understanding WHY and must come to work every day to develop the systems and hire the people who are ultimately responsible for bringing the WHY to life. The general employees are responsible for demonstrating the WHY to the outside world in whatever the company says and does. The challenge is that they are able to do it clearly.

Remember the biology of The Golden Circle. The WHY exists in the part of the brain that controls feelings and decision-making but not language. WHATs exist in the part of the brain that controls rational thought and language. Comparing the biology of the brain to the three-dimensional rendering of The Golden Circle reveals a profound insight.

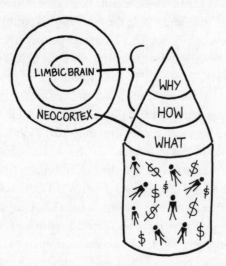

The leader sitting at the top of the organization is the inspiration, the symbol of the reason we do what we do. They represent the emotional limbic brain. WHAT the company says and does represents the rational thought and language of the neocortex. Just as it is hard for people to speak their feelings, like someone trying to explain why they love their spouse, it is equally hard for an organization to explain its WHY. The part of the brain that controls feelings and the part that controls language are not the same. Given that the cone is simply a three-dimensional rendering of The

Golden Circle, which is firmly grounded in the biology of human decision-making, the logic follows that organizations of any size will struggle to clearly communicate their WHY. Translated into business terms this means that trying to communicate your differentiating value proposition is really hard.

Put bluntly, the struggle that so many companies have to differentiate or communicate their true value to the outside world is not a business problem, it's a biology problem. And just like a person struggling to put her emotions into words, we rely on metaphors, imagery and analogies in an attempt to communicate how we feel. Absent the proper language to share our deep emotions, our purpose, cause or belief, we tell stories. We use symbols. We create tangible things for those who believe what we believe to point to and say, "That's why I'm inspired." If done properly, that's what marketing, branding and products and services become; a way for organizations to communicate to the outside world. Communicate clearly and you shall be understood.

10

COMMUNICATION IS NOT ABOUT SPEAKING, IT'S ABOUT LISTENING

Martin Luther King Jr., a man who would become a symbol of the entire civil rights movement, chose to deliver his famous "I Have a Dream" speech in front of another symbol: the Lincoln Memorial. Like King, Lincoln stands (or in the case of the memorial, sits) as a symbol of the American value of freedom for all. Great societies understand the importance of symbols as a way of reinforcing their values, of capturing their beliefs. Dictators understand the importance of symbols all too well. But in their case, the symbols are usually of them and not of a larger belief. Symbols help us make tangible that which is intangible. And the only reason symbols have meaning is because we infuse them with meaning. That meaning lives in our minds, not in the item itself. Only when the purpose, cause or belief is clear can a symbol command great power.

The flag, for example, is nothing more than a symbol of our nation's values and beliefs. And we follow the flag into battle. That's some serious power. Ever notice the patch of the American flag on a soldier's right arm? It's backward. There was no mistake made, it's like that on purpose. A flag flying on a staff, as an army was rushing into battle, would appear backward if viewed from the right side. To put it the other way around on the right shoulder would appear as if the soldier were in retreat.

Our flag is infused with so much meaning that some have tried to pass laws banning its desecration. It's not the material out of which the flag is sewn that these patriots aim to protect. The laws they propose have nothing to do with the destruction of property. Their goal is to protect the meaning the symbol represents: the WHY. The laws they drafted tried to protect the intangible set of values and beliefs by protecting the symbol of those values and beliefs. Though the laws have been struck down by the Supreme Court, they have spurred contentious and emotionally charged debates. They pit our desire for freedom of expression with our desire to protect a symbol of that freedom.

Ronald Reagan, the Great Communicator, knew all too well the power of symbols. In 1982, he was the first president to invite a "hero" to sit in the balcony of the House chamber during the State of the Union address, a tradition that has continued every year since. A man who exuded optimism, Reagan knew the value of symbolizing the values of America instead of just talking about them. His guest, who sat with the First Lady, was Lenny Skutnik, a government employee who had dived into the icy Potomac just days before to save a woman who had fallen from a helicopter that was attempting to rescue her after an Air Florida plane crashed into the river. Reagan was trying to make a point, that words are hollow, but deeds and values are deep. After he told Skutnik's story he waxed, "Don't let anyone tell you that America's best days are behind her, that the American spirit has been vanquished. We've seen it triumph too often in our lives to stop believing in it now." Skutnik became Reagan's symbol of courage.

Most companies have logos, but few have been able to convert those logos into meaningful symbols. Because most companies are bad at communicating what they believe, so it follows that most logos are devoid of any meaning. At best they serve as icons to identify a company and its products. A symbol cannot have any deep meaning until we know WHY it exists in terms bigger than simply to identify the company. Without clarity of WHY, a logo is just a logo.

To say that a logo stands for quality, service, innovation and the like only reinforces its status as just a logo. These qualities are about the company and not about the cause. Don't forget the dictators. They understand the power of symbols, except the symbols are often of them. Likewise, so many companies act like dictators—it's all about them and what they want. They tell us what to do, they tell us what we need, they tell us they have the answers but they do not inspire us and they do not command our loyalty. And to take the analogy a step further, the way dictators maintain their power is through fear, reward and every other manipulation they can think of. People follow dictators not because they want to, but because they have to. For companies to be perceived as a great leaders and not dictators, all their symbols, including their logos, need to stand for something in which we can all believe. Something we can all support. That takes clarity, discipline and consistency.

For a logo to become a symbol, people must be inspired to use that logo to say something about who they are. Couture fashion labels are the most obvious example of this. People use them to demonstrate status. But many of them are somewhat generic in what they symbolize. There is a more profound example: Harley-Davidson.

There are people who walk around with Harley-Davidson tattoos on their bodies. That's insane. They've tattooed a corporate logo on their skin. Some of them don't even own the product! Why would rational people tattoo a corporate logo on their bodies? The reason is simple. After years of Harley being crystal clear about what they believe, after years of being disciplined about a set of values and guiding principles and after years of being doggedly consistent about everything they say and do, their logo has become a symbol. It no longer simply identifies a company and its products; it identifies a belief.

In truth, most people who tattoo Harley-Davidson logos on their bodies have no idea what the stock price of Harley is. They have no idea about some management shake-up the week before. That symbol is no longer about Harley. The logo embodies an entire value set—their own. The symbol is no longer about Harley, it's about them. Randy Fowler, a former U.S. Marine and now general manager of a Harley-Davidson dealership in California, proudly sports a large Harley tattoo on his left arm. "It symbolizes who I am," he says. "Mostly, it says I'm an American." Customer and company are now one and the same. The meaning of Harley-Davidson has value in people's lives because, for those who believe in Harley's WHY, it helps them express the meaning of their own lives.

Because of Harley's clarity, discipline and consistency, most will know what that symbol means, even if you don't subscribe to it yourself. That's the reason why when someone walks into a bar with a big Harley logo on his arm we take a step back and give him a wide berth. The symbol has become so meaningful, in fact, that 12 percent of Harley-Davidson revenues are strictly from merchandising. That's remarkable.

It's not just logos, however, that can serve as symbols. Symbols are any tangible representation of a clear set of values and beliefs. An ink-stained finger for Iraqis was a symbol of a new beginning. A London double-decker bus or a cowboy hat—both are symbols of national cultures. But national symbols are easy because most nations have a clear sense of culture that has been reinforced and repeated for generations. It is not a company or organization that decides what, it symbols mean, it is the group outside the megaphone, in the chaotic marketplace, who decide. If, based on the things they see and hear, the outsiders can clearly and consistently report what an organization believes, then, and only then, can a symbol start to take on meaning. It is the truest test of how effective a megaphone has been produced—when clarity is able to filter all the way through the organization and come to life in everything that comes out of it.

Go back to Apple's "1984" commercial at the beginning of chapter 9. For those who have seen it, does it make you think about Apple and its products or do you simply like the sentiment? Or the line "Think Different," does it speak to you?

If you're a Mac customer, you probably loved this commercial;

it may even give you goose bumps when you watch it—a surefire test that the WHY is connecting with you on a visceral or limbic level. In fact, this commercial, after you learned it was from Apple, may have reinforced your decision to buy a Mac, whether for the first time or the tenth time. This commercial, like all Apple's advertising, is one of the things Apple has said or done that reinforces what they believe. It is every bit consistent with the clear belief we know they embody. And if the commercial speaks to you and you're not an Apple lover, odds are you still like the idea of thinking differently. The message of that ad is one of the things Apple does to tell their story. It is one of the WHATs to their WHY. It is a symbol. It is for these reasons that we say of a piece of advertising, "It really speaks to me." It's not really speaking to you, it's speaking to the millions of people who saw the ad. When we say that something like that "speaks to me," what we're really saying is, through all this clutter and noise, I can hear that. I can hear it and I will listen. This is what it means for a message that comes out of the megaphone to resonate.

Everything that comes out of the base of the megaphone serves as a way for an organization to articulate what it believes. What a company says and does are the means by which the company speaks. Too many companies put a disproportionate amount of weight on their products or services simply because those are the things that bring in the money. But there are many more things at the base of the megaphone that play an equal role in speaking to the outside world. Though products may drive sales, they alone cannot create loyalty. In fact, a company can create loyalty among people who aren't even customers. I spoke favorably of Apple long before I bought one. And I spoke disparagingly of a certain PC brand even though I'd been buying their products for years.

Apple's clarity, discipline and consistency—their ability to build a megaphone, not a company, that is clear and loud—is what has given them the ability to command such loyalty. They are accused of having a cultlike following. Those inside the company are often accused of following the "cult of Steve." All of these compliments or insults are indications that others have taken on the cause and made it their own. That experts describe their products and marketing as a "lifestyle" reinforces that people who love Apple products are using WHAT Apple does to demonstrate their own personal identity. We call it "lifestyle marketing" because people have integrated commercial products into the style of their lives. Apple, with great efficiency, built a perfectly clear megaphone, leveraged the Law of Diffusion and invited others to help spread the gospel. Not for the company, for themselves.

Even their promotions and partnerships serve as tangible proof of what they believe. In 2003 and 2004, Apple ran a promotion for iTunes with Pepsi—the cola branded as "the choice of the next generation." It made sense that Apple would do a deal with Pepsi, the primary challenger to Coca-Cola, the status quo. Everything Apple does, everything they say and do, serves as tangible proof of what they believe. The reason I use Apple so extensively throughout this book is that Apple is so disciplined in HOW they do things and so consistent in WHAT they do that, love them or hate them, we all have a sense of their WHY. We know what they believe.

Most of us didn't read books about them. We didn't personally know Steve Jobs. We haven't spent time roaming the halls of Apple's headquarters to get to know their culture. The clarity we have for what Apple believes comes from one place and one place only: Apple. People don't buy WHAT you do, they buy WHY you do it, and Apple says and does only the things they believe. If WHAT you do doesn't prove what you believe, then no one will know what your WHY is and you'll be forced to compete on price, service, quality, features and benefits; the stuff of commodities. Apple has a clear and loud megaphone and is exceptionally good at communicating his story.

The Celery Test

In order to improve HOW and WHAT we do, we constantly look to what others are doing. We attend conferences, read books, talk to friends and colleagues to get their input and advice, and some-times we are also the dispensers of advice. We are in pursuit of understanding the best practices of others to help guide us. But it is a flawed assumption that what works for one organization will work for another. Even if the industries, sizes and market condi-tions are the same, the notion that "if it's good for them, it's good for us" is simply not true.

I know of a company with an amazing culture. When asked, the employees say they love that all the conference rooms have ping-pong tables in them. Does that mean that if you were to put ping-pong tables in all your conference rooms your culture would improve? Of course not. But this is an example of "best practices." The idea that copying WHAT or HOW things are done at high-performing organizations will inherently work for you is just not true. Like the Ferrari and the Honda, what is good for one company is not necessarily good for another. Put simply, best prac-tices are not always best.

It is not just WHAT or HOW you do things that matters; what matters more is that WHAT and HOW you do things is consistent with your WHY. Only then will your practices indeed be best. There is nothing inherently wrong with looking to others to learn what they do, the challenge is knowing what practices or advice to fol-low. Fortunately, there is a simple test you can apply to find out exactly WHAT and HOW is right for you. It's a simple metaphor called the Celery Test.

Imagine you go to a dinner party and somebody comes up to you and says, "You know what you need in your organization? M&M's. If you're not using M&M's in your business, you're leaving money on the table."

Somebody else comes up to you and says, "You know what you need? Rice milk. The data shows that all the people are buy-ing rice milk these days. You should be selling rice milk in this economy."

While you're standing over the punch bowl, yet another person offers some sage advice. "Oreo cookies," he says. "We made millions from implementing Oreo cookies in our organization. You've got to do it."

Still somebody else comes up to you and says, "Celery. You've got to get into celery."

You get all this great advice from all these highly accomplished people. Some of them are in the same industry. Some of them are more successful than you. Some of them have offered similar advice to others with great success. Now, what do you do?

You go to the supermarket and you buy celery, rice milk, Oreos and M&M's. You spend a lot of time at the supermarket walking the aisles. You spend a lot of money because you buy everything. But you may or may not get any value from some or all of these products; there are no guarantees. Worse, if you're budget-constrained, you had to whittle down your choices again. And then which do you choose?

But one thing's for sure: when you're standing in line at the supermarket with all of these items in your arms, your celery, rice milk, Oreos and M&Ms, nobody can see what you believe. What you do is supposed serve as the tangible proof of what you believe, and you bought everything.

But what if you knew your WHY before you went to the supermarket? What if your WHY is to do only things that are healthy? To always do the things that are good for your body? You'll get all the same good advice from all the same people, the only difference is, the next time you go to the supermarket, you'll buy only rice milk and celery. Those are the only products that make sense. It's not that the other advice isn't good advice, it's just not good for you. The advice doesn't fit.

Filtering your decisions through your WHY, you spend less time at the supermarket and you spend less money, so there's an efficiency advantage also. You're guaranteed to get value out of all the products you bought. And, most importantly, when you're standing in line with your products in your arms, everybody can see what you believe. With only celery and rice milk it's obvious to people walking by what you believe. "I can *see* that you believe in looking after your health," they may say to you. "I feel the same way. I have a question for you." Congratulations. You just attracted a customer, an employee, a partner or a referral simply by making the right decisions. Simply ensuring that WHAT you do proves what you believe makes it easy for those who believe what you believe to find you. You have successfully communicated your WHY based on WHAT you do.

This is an idealistic concept and in the real world that level of discipline is not always possible. I understand that sometimes we have to make short-term decisions to pay bills or get some short-term advantage. That's fine. The Celery Test still applies. If you want a piece of chocolate cake, go right ahead. The difference is, when you start with WHY, you know full well that the chocolate cake is a short-term decision that doesn't fit with your beliefs. You're under no illusions. You know you are only doing it for the short-term sugar rush and you'll have to work a little harder to get it out of your system. It's astounding the number of businesses I see that view an opportunity as the one that's going to set them on a path to glory, only to have it blow up or slowly deflate over time. They see the chocolate cake and can't resist. Starting with WHY not only helps you know which is the right advice for you to follow, but also to know which decisions will put you out of balance. You can certainly make those decisions if you need to, but don't make too many of them, otherwise over time, no one will know what you believe.

But here's the best part. As soon as I told you the WHY, you knew that we were going to buy only celery and rice milk even before you read it. As soon as I gave you the filter, as soon as I said the WHY, you knew exactly what decisions to make before I said so.

That's called scale.

With a WHY clearly stated in an organization, anyone within the organization can make a decision as clearly and as accurately as the founder. A WHY provides the clear filter for decision-making. Any decisions—hiring, partnerships, strategies and tactics—should all pass the Celery Test.

The More Celery You Use, the More Trust You Earn

Mark Rubin is a good parent. He spends a lot of time with his two daughters, Lucy and Sophie. One Saturday afternoon, his wife, Claudine, took Lucy to a friend's for a playdate and Mark was left home to look after five-year-old Sophie. Feeling a little tired, Mark really wanted to just have a little time to relax on the couch and not have to play tree house again for the ninth time that day. To keep Sophie occupied, he opted for the TV as babysitter. Mark had two brand-new DVDs to choose from. He'd seen neither of them and heard nothing about either of them in the press or from any of his friends with small children. Mark didn't feel like watching the cartoon himself—the plan was to let Sophie enjoy the movie in one room while he watched something in the other room. One of the DVDs was from some company he'd never heard of and the other was from Disney. Which one did he put in the DVD player? Which one would you put in the DVD player?

The answer is so clear it verges on a silly question, but let's consider the facts for fun. Both DVDs were cartoons. Both were age-appropriate for a child. Both had a couple of good reviews on the packaging. The only difference is that we trust the DVD from Disney. Disney is not a perfect company. They occasionally have management and leadership issues. Their stock price sometimes goes down. They have lawsuits filed against them all the time. Some would lump them in with all the other nasty corporations that work to appease Wall Street. So why would we trust them?

Disney operates with a clear sense of WHY—they exist to promote good, clean family fun and everything they say and do has, for decades, worked to prove it. The reason we trust Disney is simple; we know what they believe. They pass the Celery Test. They have been so consistent over time in everything they say and do that parents trust them enough to expose their children to Disney content without vetting it first. This has nothing to do with quality products. This is not rational.

Southwest Airlines also passes the Celery Test. The company has been so consistent over time that we almost know what to expect from them. The airline offers only open seating on its flights, for example. It's one of the things they do to prove that they believe in freedom. It just makes sense. A company that serves the common man and values equality for all so much could never have a class structure. If Delta or United or Continental tried to do the same, it wouldn't make sense, open seating doesn't fit their way.

In Violation of Celery

Birkenstock sandals, tie-dyed T-shirts, daisy chains and a VW van. All are symbols of the hippie ideals of peace, love and all things vegetarian. So it was a bit of a surprise in 2004 when Volkswagen introduced a $70,000 luxury model to their lineup. The company famous for putting a vase for fresh flowers on the dashboard of their new Beetle introduced the Phaeton in an attempt to compete with high-end luxury cars, including the Mercedes-Benz S-Class and the BMW 7 Series. The V-8, 335-horsepower car boasted some of the most advanced features in the industry, like an air compressor suspension system and a draftless four-zone climate control. It even included an electronically controlled shiatsu massage system in the seats. The car was an astounding achievement. It was very comfortable and was a monster on the road, outperforming other more established luxury cars in its class. The critics loved it. But there was a small problem. Despite all the facts and figures, features and benefits, and regardless of the world-renowned German engineering, few people bought one. It just didn't make sense. What VW had done was inconsistent with what we knew them to believe.

Volkswagen, which translated means "people's car," had spent generations making cars for you and me. Everyone knew what VW stood for—power to the people. It brought its cause to life in products that were all about quality that the average person could afford. In a single swoop of German ingenuity, VW had been put completely out of balance. This is not like Dell coming out with an mp3 player or United starting the low-cost airline Ted. In those cases, we had no idea what the companies' WHYs were. Absent any knowledge or feeling for their WHY, we couldn't bring ourselves to buy products from them that went anything beyond WHAT they do. In this case, VW has a clear WHY, but WHAT they produced was completely misaligned. They failed the Celery Test.

Toyota and Honda knew this better than Volkswagen. When they decided to add luxury models to their lineups, they created new brands, Lexus and Acura, respectively, to do it. Toyota had become a symbol of efficiency and affordability to the general population. They had built their business on a suite of low-cost cars. They knew that the market would not pay a premium for a luxury car with the same name or with the same logo on the hood. Although a luxury car, Lexus is still another WHAT to Toyota's WHY. It still embodies the same cause as the Toyota-branded cars, and the values of the company are the same. The only difference is WHAT they are doing to bring that cause to life.

The good news is, VW hasn't made the same mistake again, and their WHY remains clear. But if a company tries too many times to "seize market opportunities" inconsistent with their WHY over time, their WHY will go fuzzy and their ability to inspire and command loyalty will deteriorate.

What companies say and do matters. A lot. It is at the WHAT level that a cause is brought to life. It is at this level that a company speaks to the outside world and it is then that we can learn what the company believes.

PART 5

THE BIGGEST
CHALLENGE
IS SUCCESS

11

WHEN WHY GOES FUZZY

Goliath Flinched

"A lot of what goes on these days with high-flying companies and these overpaid CEOs, who're really just looting from the top and aren't watching out for anybody but themselves, really upsets me. It's one of the main things wrong with American business today." This is the sentiment passed down from the founder of one of the most vilified companies in recent history.

Raised on a farm in America's heartland, he came of age during the Great Depression. This probably explained his predisposition for frugality. Standing five feet nine inches and weighing only 130 pounds when he played football in high school, Sam Walton, the founder of Wal-Mart, learned early the value of working hard. Working hard leads to winning. And as the quarterback on his high school football team, he won a lot. In fact, they went on to become state champs. Whether through hard work, luck or just an unflappable optimism, Walton got so used to winning all the time that he couldn't fully visualize what losing looked like. He simply couldn't imagine it. Walton even philosophized that always thinking about winning probably became a self-fulfilling prophecy for him. Even during the Depression, he had a highly successful paper route that earned him a decent wage for the times.

By the time Sam Walton died, he had taken Wal-Mart from a single store in Bentonville, Arkansas, and turned it into a retail colossus with $44 billion in annual sales with 40 million people shopping in the stores per week. But it takes more than a competitive nature, a strong work ethic and a sense of optimism to build a company big enough to equal the twenty-third-largest economy in the world.

Walton wasn't the first person with big dreams to start a small business. Many small business owners dream of making it big. I meet a lot of entrepreneurs and it is amazing how many of them tell me their goal is to build a billion-dollar company. The odds, however, are significantly stacked against them. There are 27.7 million registered businesses in the United States today and only a thousand of them get to be FORTUNE 1000 companies, which these days requires about $1.5 billion in annual revenues. That means that less than .004 percent of all companies make it to the illustrious list. To have such an impact, to build a company to a size where it can drive markets, requires something more.

Sam Walton did not invent the low-cost shopping model. The five-and-dime variety store concept had existed for decades and Kmart and Target opened their doors the same year as Wal-Mart, in 1962. Discounting was already a $2 billion industry when Walton decided to build his first Wal-Mart. There was plenty of competition beyond Kmart and Target, some of it much better funded and with better locations and seemingly better opportunities for success than Wal-Mart. Sam Walton didn't even invent a better way of doing things than everyone else. He admitted to "borrowing" many of his ideas about the business from Sol Price, the founder of Fed-Mart, a retail discounter founded in Southern California during the 1950s.

Wal-Mart was not the only retail establishment capable of offering low prices either. Price, as we've already established, is a highly effective manipulation. But it alone does not inspire people to root for you and give you the undying loyalty needed to create a tipping point to grow to massive proportions. Being cheap does not inspire employees to give their blood, sweat and tears. Wal-Mart did not have a lock on cheap prices and cheap prices are not what made it so beloved and ultimately so successful.

For Sam Walton, there was something else, a deeper purpose, cause or belief that drove him. More than anything else, Walton believed in people. He believed that if he looked after people, people would look after him. The more Wal-Mart could give to employees, customers and the community, the more that employees, customers and the community would give back to Wal-Mart. "We're all working together; that's the secret," said Walton.

This was a much bigger concept than simply "passing on the savings." To Walton, the inspiration came not simply from customer service but from service itself. Wal-Mart was WHAT Walton built to serve his fellow human beings. To serve the community, to serve employees and to serve customers. Service was a higher cause.

The problem was that his cause was not clearly handed down after he died. In the post-Sam era, Wal-Mart slowly started to confuse WHY it existed—to serve people—with HOW it did business—to offer low prices. They traded the inspiring cause of serving people for a manipulation. They forgot Walton's WHY and their driving motivation became all about "cheap." In stark contrast to the founding cause that Wal-Mart originally embodied, efficiency and margins became the name of the game. "A computer can tell you down to the dime what you've sold, but it can never tell you how much you could have sold," said Walton. There is always a price to pay for the money you make, and given Wal-Mart's sheer size, that cost wasn't paid in dollars and cents alone. In Wal-Mart's case, forgetting their founder's WHY has come at a very high human cost. Ironic, considering the company's founding cause.

The company once renowned for how it treated employees and customers has been scandal-ridden for nearly a decade. Nearly every scandal has centered on how poorly they treat their customers and their employees. As of December 2008, Wal-Mart faced seventy-three class-action lawsuits related to wage violations and has already paid hundreds of millions of dollars in past judgments and settlements. A company that believed in the symbiotic relationship between corporation and community managed to drive a wedge between themselves and so many of the communities in which they operate. There was a time when legislators would help pass laws to allow Wal-Mart into new communities; now lawmakers rally to keep them out. Fights to block Wal-Mart from opening new stores have erupted across the country. In New York, for example, city representatives in Brooklyn joined forces with labor unions to block the store because of Wal-Mart's reputation for unfair labor practices.

In one of the more ironic violations of Walton's founding beliefs, Wal-Mart has been unable to laugh at itself or learn from its scandals. "Celebrate your successes," said Walton. "Find some humor in your failures. Don't take yourself so seriously. Loosen up and everybody around you will loosen up." Instead of admitting that things aren't what they used to be, Wal-Mart has done the opposite.

The way Wal-Mart thinks, acts and communicates since the passing of their inspired leader is not a result of their competitors outsmarting them either. Kmart filed for Chapter 11 bankruptcy protection in 2002, and then merged with Sears three years later. With about $400 billion in annual sales, Wal-Mart still sells more than six times as much as Target each year. In fact, looking beyond discount retailing, Wal-Mart is now the largest supermarket in the world and sells more DVDs, bicycles and toys than any other company in America. Outside competition is not what's hurting the company. The greatest challenge Wal-Mart has faced over the years comes from one place: itself.

For Wal-Mart, WHAT they do and HOW they are doing it hasn't changed. And it has nothing to do with Wal-Mart being a "corporation"; they were one of those before the love started to decline. What has changed is that their WHY went fuzzy. And we all know it. A company once so loved is simply not as loved anymore. The negative feelings we have for the company are real, but the part of the brain that is able to explain why we feel so negatively toward them has trouble explaining what changed. So we rationalize and point to the most tangible things we can see—size and money. If we, as outsiders, have lost clarity of Wal-Mart's WHY, it's a good sign that the WHY has gone fuzzy inside the company also. If it's not clear on the inside, it will never be clear on the outside. What is clear is that the Wal-Mart of today is not the Wal-Mart that Sam Walton built. So what happened?

It's too easy to say that all they care about is their bottom line. All companies are in business to make money, but being successful at it is not the reason why things change so drastically. That only points to a symptom. Without understanding the reason it happened in the first place, the pattern will repeat for every other company that makes it big. It is not destiny or some mystical business cycle that transforms successful companies into impersonal goliaths. It's people.

Being Successful vs. Feeling Successful

Every year a group of high-performing entrepreneurs get together at MIT's Endicott House just outside Boston. This Gathering of Titans, as they call themselves, is not your average entrepreneurial conference. It's not a boondoggle. There's no golf, there's no spa and there are no expensive dinners. Every year forty to fifty business owners spend four days listening, from early in the morning until well into the evening. An assortment of guest speakers is invited to present their thinking and ideas, and then there are discussions led by some of the attendees.

I had the honor of attending the Gathering of Titans as a guest a few years ago. I expected it to be another group of entrepreneurs getting together to talk shop. I expected to hear discussions and presentations about maximizing profits and improving systems. But what I witnessed was profoundly different. In fact, it was the complete opposite.

On the first day, someone asked the group how many of them had achieved their financial goals. About 80 percent of the hands went up. I thought that alone was quite impressive. But it was the answer to the next question that was so profound. With their hands still in the air, the group was then asked, "How many of you feel successful?" And 80 percent of the hands went down.

Here was a room full of some of America's brightest entrepreneurs, many of them multimillionaires, some of whom don't need to work anymore if they don't want to, yet most of them still didn't feel like they had succeeded. In fact, many of them reported that they'd lost something since they started their businesses. They reminisced about the days when they didn't have any money and were working out of their basements, trying to get things going. They longed for the feeling they used to have.

These amazing entrepreneurs were at a point in their lives where they realized that their businesses were about much more than selling stuff or making money. They realized the deep personal connection that existed between WHAT they do and WHY they were doing it. This group of entrepreneurs gathered to discuss matters of WHY, and at times it was quite intense.

Unlike the typical type A–personality entrepreneurs, the Titans were not there to prove anything to each other. There was a feeling of immense trust rather than ruthless competition. And because of this feeling, every member of the group was willing to express vulnerability that they probably rarely let show the rest of the year. Over the course of the event, every person in the room would shed a tear or two at least once.

It doesn't interest me to write about the idea that money doesn't buy happiness or, in this case, the feeling of success. This is neither profound nor a new idea. What does interest me, however, is the transition that these entrepreneurs went through. As their companies grew, and they became more and more successful, what changed?

It is easy to see what they gained over the course of their careers—we can easily count the money, the size of the office, the number of employees, the size of their homes, market share and the number of press clippings. But the thing they had lost is much harder to identify. As their tangible success grew, something more elusive started to dissipate. Every single one of these successful business owners knew WHAT they did. They knew HOW they did it. But for many, they no longer knew WHY.

Achievement vs. Success

For some people, there is an irony to success. Many people who achieve great success don't always feel it. Some who achieve fame talk about the loneliness that often goes with it. That's because success and achievement are not the same thing, yet too often we mistake one for the other. Achievement is something you reach or attain, like a goal. It is something tangible, clearly defined and measurable. Success, in contrast, is a feeling or a state of being. "She feels successful. She *is* successful," we say, using the verb *to be* to suggest this state of *being*. While we can easily lay down a path to reach a goal, laying down a path to reach that intangible feeling of success is more elusive. In my vernacular, achievement comes when you pursue and attain WHAT you want. Success comes when you are clear in pursuit of WHY you want it. The former is motivated by tangible factors while the latter by something deeper in the brain, where we lack the capacity to put those feelings into words.

Success comes when we wake up every day in that never-ending pursuit of WHY we do WHAT we do. Our achievements, WHAT we do, serve as the milestones to indicate we are on the right path. It is not an either/or—we need both. A wise man once said, "Money can't buy happiness, but it pays for the yacht to pull alongside it." There is great truth in this statement. The yacht represents achievement; it is easily seen and, with the right plan, completely attainable. The thing we pull alongside represents that hard-to-define feeling of success. Obviously, this is much harder to see and attain. They are distinct concepts, and sometimes they go together and sometimes they don't. More importantly, some people, while in pursuit of success, simply mistake WHAT they achieve as the final destination. This is the reason they never feel satisfied no matter how big their yacht is, no matter how much they achieve. The false assumption we often make is that if we simply achieve more, the feeling of success will follow. But it rarely does.

In the course of building a business or a career, we become more confident in WHAT we do. We become greater experts in HOW to do it. With each achievement, the tangible measurements of success and the feeling of progress increase. Life is good. However, for most of us, somewhere in the journey we forget WHY we set out on the journey in the first place. Somewhere in the course of all those achievements an inevitable split happens. This is true for individuals and organizations alike. What the Endicott entrepreneurs experienced as individuals was the same transition that Wal-Mart and other big companies either have gone through or are going through. Because Wal-Mart operates at such an immense scale, the impact of their fuzzy WHY is felt on a greater scale. Employees, customers and the community will feel it also.

Those with an ability to never lose sight of WHY, no matter how little or how much they achieve, can inspire us. Those with the ability to never lose sight of WHY and also achieve the milestones that keep everyone focused in the right direction are the great leaders. For great leaders, The Golden Circle is in balance. They are in pursuit of WHY, they hold themselves accountable to HOW they do it and WHAT they do serves as the tangible proof of what they believe. But most of us, unfortunately, reach a place where WHAT we are doing and WHY we are doing it eventually fall out of balance. We get to a point when WHY and WHAT are not aligned. It is the separation of the tangible and the intangible that marks the split.

12

SPLIT HAPPENS

Wal-Mart started small. So did Microsoft. So did Apple. So did General Electric and Ford and almost every other company that made it big. They didn't start by acquisition or spin-off, or achieve mass scale overnight. Nearly every company or organization starts the same way: with an idea. No matter whether an organization grows to become a multibillion-dollar corporation like Wal-Mart or fails in the first few years, most of them started with a single person or small group of people who had an idea. Even the United States of America started the same way.

At the beginning, ideas are fueled by passion—that very compelling emotion that causes us to do quite irrational things. That passion drives many people to make sacrifices so that a cause bigger than themselves can be brought to life. Some drop out of school or quit a perfectly good job with a good salary and benefits to try to go it alone. Some work extraordinarily long hours without a second thought, sometimes sacrificing the stability of their relationships or even their personal health. This passion is so intoxicating and exciting that it can affect others as well. Inspired by the founder's vision, many early employees demonstrate classic early-adopter behavior. Relying on their gut, these first employees also quit their perfectly good jobs and accept lower salaries to join an organization with a 90 percent statistical chance of failing. But the statistics don't matter; passion and optimism reign and energy is high. Like all early adopters, the behavior of those who join early says more about them than it does about the company's prospects.

The reason so many small businesses fail, however, is because passion alone can't cut it. For passion to survive, it needs structure. A WHY without the HOWs, passion without structure, has a very high probability of failure. Remember the dot-com boom? Lots of passion, but not so much structure. The Titans at Endicott House, however, did not face this problem. They knew how to build the systems and processes to see their companies grow. They are among the statistical 10 percent of small businesses that didn't fail in their first three years. In fact, many of them went on to do quite well. Their challenge was different. Passion may need structure to survive, but for structure to grow, it needs passion.

This is what I witnessed at the Gathering of Titans: I saw a room full of people with passion enough to start businesses, and with knowledge enough to build the systems and structures to survive and even do very well. But having spent so many years focused on converting a vision into a viable business, many started to fixate on WHAT the organization did or HOW to do it. Poring over financials or some other easily measured result, and fixating on HOW they were to achieve those tangible results, they stopped focusing on WHY they started the business in the first place. This is also what has happened at Wal-Mart. A company obsessed with serving the community became obsessed with achieving its goals.

Like Wal-Mart, the Endicott entrepreneurs used to think, act and communicate from the inside out of The Golden Circle—from WHY to WHAT. But as they grew more successful, the process reversed. WHAT now comes first and all their systems and processes are in pursuit of those tangible results. The reason the change happened is simple—they suffered a split and their WHY went fuzzy.

The Biggest Challenge Is Success

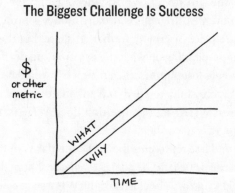

The single greatest challenge any organization will face is . . . success. When the company is small, the founder will rely on his gut to make all the major decisions. From marketing to product, from strategy to tactics, hiring and firing, the decisions the founder makes will, if he trusts his gut, feel right. But as the organization grows, as it becomes more successful, it becomes physically impossible for one person to make every major decision. Not only must others be trusted and relied upon to make big decisions, but those people will also start making hiring choices. And slowly but surely, as the megaphone grows, the clarity of WHY starts to dilute.

Whereas gut was the filter for early decisions, rational cases and empirical data often serve as the sole basis for later decisions. For all organizations that go through the split, they are no longer inspired by a cause greater than themselves. They simply come to work, manage systems and work to reach certain preset goals. There is no longer a cathedral to build. The passion is gone and inspiration is at a minimum. At that point, for most who show up every day what they do is just a job. If this is how the people on the inside feel, imagine how those on the outside feel. It is no wonder that manipulations start to dominate not only how the company sells its wares, but even how they retain employees. Bonuses, promotions and other enticements, even instilling fear in people, become the only way to hold on to talent. That's hardly inspiring.

This diagram depicts the life of an organization. The top line represents the growth of WHAT the organization does. For a company, that measurement is usually money—profits, revenues, EBITA, share price or growth in market share. But the metric can be anything, depending on what the organization does. If the organization rescues lost puppies, then the metric would be the number of puppies successfully rescued. It is inherently simple to measure the growth of WHAT an organization does. WHATs, after all, are tangible and easy to count.

The second line represents the WHY, the clarity of the founding purpose, cause or belief. The goal is to ensure that as the measurement of WHAT grows, the clarity of the WHY stays closely aligned. Put another way, as the volume of the megaphone increases, the message traveling through it must stay clear.

The volume of the megaphone comes solely from growth of WHAT. As this metric grows, any company can become a "leading" company. But it is the ability to inspire, to maintain clarity of WHY, that gives only a few people and organizations the ability to lead. The moment at which the clarity of WHY starts to go fuzzy is the split. At this point organizations may be loud, but they are no longer clear.

When organizations are small, WHAT they do and WHY they do it are in close parallel. Born out of the personality of the founder, it is relatively easy for early employees to "get it." Clarity of WHY is understood because the source of passion is near—in fact it physically comes to work every day. In most small businesses all the employees are all crammed into the same room and socialize together. Simply being around a charismatic founder allows that feeling of being a part of something special to flourish. Although there may be some efficiencies to be gained, for small businesses that are perfectly comfortable staying small, the need to articulate the WHY is not as important. For organizations that want to pass the School Bus Test, to become billion-dollar organizations or work at a scale large enough to shift markets or society, the need to manage through the split is paramount.

The School Bus Test is a simple metaphor. If a founder or leader of an organization were to be hit by a school bus, would the organization continue to thrive at the same pace without them at the helm? So many organizations are built on the force of a single personality that their departure can cause significant disruption. The question isn't if it happens—all founders eventually leave or die—it's just a question of when and how prepared the organization is for the inevitable departure. The challenge isn't to cling to the leader, it's to find effective ways to keep the founding vision alive forever.

To pass the School Bus Test, for an organization to continue to inspire and lead beyond the lifetime of its founder, the founder's WHY must be extracted and integrated into the culture of the company. What's more, a strong succession plan should aim to find a leader inspired by the founding cause and ready to lead it into the next generation. Future leaders and employees alike must be inspired by something bigger than the force of personality of the founder and must see beyond profit and shareholder value alone.

Microsoft has experienced a split, but is not so far down the line that it can't be put back on track. There was a time not too long ago that people at Microsoft showed up at work every day to change the world. And they did. What Microsoft achieved, putting a PC on every desk, dramatically changed the way we live. But then their WHY went fuzzy. Few people at the company today are instructed to do everything they can to help people be more productive so that they can achieve their greatest potential. Instead, Microsoft became just a software company.

If you visit Microsoft's headquarters in Redmond, Washington, you will find that although their WHY has gone fuzzy, it is not lost. That sense of a cause, that desire to change the world again, is still there, but it has become unfocused, wrapped up in HOW and WHAT they do. Microsoft has a remarkable opportunity to clarify their WHY and regain the inspiration that took them to where they are today. If they do not, if all they do is manage the WHAT and continue to ignore the WHY, they will end up looking like America Online, a company so far past the split that their WHY is indeed lost. There is barely a hint of the original WHY left anymore.

America Online used to inspire. Like Google today, it was the hot company to work for. People clamored to move to Virginia to work for this amazing company that was changing the rules of business. And it was true that, like all inspiring companies, AOL set in motion changes that profoundly altered how we do almost everything. They inspired a nation to get online. Their cause was clear and their decisions were governed by their WHY. Their goal was to get more people online, even if their decisions in pursuit of that goal wreaked havoc on their business in the short term. With their WHY in focus, AOL pulled ahead of their competition by deciding to change from hourly pricing for Internet access to unlimited monthly pricing, a decision that created so much traffic it shut down their servers. Given the impact, the decision was neither practical nor rational, but it was the right choice to help bring their cause to life. That their systems shut down with the additional traffic only pushed them to work harder to cope with it, to ensure that America could, in fact, get and stay online.

In those days, having an AOL e-mail address was a point of pride—a sign of being one of those who was a part of the Internet revolution. These days, still having an AOL e-mail address is a symbol of having been left behind. That the meaning of something as simple as @*aol.com* has changed so dramatically is additional proof that the company's cause has long since departed. Absent a clear WHY, size and momentum are all AOL has to keep them going. The company is not inspiring anymore, not to those who work there and not to those on the outside. We don't talk about them like we used to and we certainly don't feel the same way about them either. We don't compare them to Google or Facebook or any of the other industry-changing companies of today. Like a massive freight train with brakes applied, it will still take miles for this train to come to a complete stop. It's simple physics. At best AOL's size will help them putter along, but without a more compelling purpose, cause or belief, the company is simply a collection of stuff. It will probably end up being chopped up and sold off for scrap (technology or customers), which is a sad reality considering how inspiring AOL used to be.

It is not a coincidence that successful entrepreneurs long for the early days. It is no accident that big companies talk about a "return to basics." What they are alluding to is a time before the split. And they would be right. They do indeed need to return to a time when WHAT they did was in perfect parallel to WHY they did it. If they continue down the path of focusing on their growth of WHAT at the expense of WHY—more volume and less clarity—their ability to thrive and inspire for years to come is dubious at best. Companies like Wal-Mart, Microsoft, Starbucks, the Gap, Dell and so many others that used to be special have all gone through a split. If they cannot recapture their WHY and reinspire those inside and outside their organization, every one of them will end up looking more like AOL than the companies they were.

What Gets Measured, Gets Done

In the fall of her freshman year in college, Christina Harbridge set out to find a part-time job. Intrigued by the prospect of working in the antiques business, she answered a newspaper ad in Sacramento to do office work for a "collector." Harbridge soon found out, however, that the job was filing papers for a collections agent, and even then she wasn't entirely sure what that meant.

The collections office consisted of a huge room with dozens of phone stations, each staffed by a debt collector making call after call to a long list of businesses and individuals who owed money. The setup of the room meant there was no privacy—everyone could hear everyone else's calls. Harbridge was immediately taken by the harshness of the tone that all the collectors used with those from whom they aimed to collect unpaid debts. "They would hound them, and practically threaten them," she said. "They would do anything it took to get information from them."

Harbridge recognized that the owner of the company and the collectors were all kind, gracious people. They helped each other out, listened to each other's problems and even joined together to sponsor a homeless family during the holidays. But when they were on the phone to collect a debt, these same people turned passive-aggressive, rude and often mean. It's not because they were bad people, it's because they were incentivized to be that way.

Their officious behavior made perfect sense. "What gets measured gets done," as well-known sales coach Jack Daly says. And in the world of debt collecting, the callers were given bonuses based on how much money they collected. This has resulted in an entire industry that threatens, badgers, hounds and provokes. It didn't take long until Harbridge found herself adopting the same attitude whenever she talked with debtors. "I began treating people on the phone the way everybody else in the office treated them," she said.

Feeling like WHAT she was doing was completely out of balance with her WHY, Harbridge decided there had to be another way. "I got it in my head that I was going to start an agency that collected by being nice," she said. People in the collections business thought Harbridge naïve, if not crazy. And maybe she was.

In 1993, Harbridge moved to San Francisco and started her own collections firm, Bridgeport Financial, steeped in the belief that agents would have more success treating people with respect than badgering them. Harbridge built her company on her WHY— that everyone has a story and everyone deserves to be listened to. Her approach was to have her agents try to establish rapport with the debtor on the other end of the phone in the course of a three-minute conversation. The goal was to learn everything they could about the person's circumstances: Did they have the means to pay the debt? Would they honor a payment plan? Was the reason for the failure to pay reflective of a short-term situation? "We would get people to tell us the truth," she said. "Sure, we had a legal department, but we tried to avoid using it." Harbridge knew, however, that no matter her intentions, if she measured the results the same way as others, the same awful behavior would result. So she came up with an entirely new way to incentivize her people. She found a way to measure WHY.

At Bridgeport Financial, bonuses were not given for the amount of money that was collected; they were given based on how many "thank you" cards her agents sent out. This is harder than it sounds. Sending out a card thanking someone for the time they spent talking on the phone requires a few things. First, Harbridge had to hire people who believed what she believed. She had to hire good fits. If her employees didn't believe that everyone deserves to be listened to, it wouldn't work. Only good-fit hires would be capable of creating an environment on the telephone that would actually warrant sending a thank-you card, even though the purpose of the call was to ask for money. Harbridge measured WHY her company existed, not WHAT they did, and the result was a culture in which compassion was valued above all.

But what about the other results? What about her financial results, the ones most businesses pursue first? Bridgeport Financial collected 300 percent more than the industry average. What's more, most of the people and companies who were initially being pursued ended up doing more business with the original company that sent the collections agency after them in the first place. This is almost unprecedented in the collections industry.

Harbridge's business succeeded not just because she knew WHY she was doing what she was doing, but because she found a way to measure the WHY. The company's growth was loud and her cause was clear. She started with WHY and the rest followed.

Most organizations today use very clear metrics to track the progress and growth of WHAT they do—usually it's money. Unfortunately, we have very poor measurements to ensure that a WHY stays clear. Dwayne Honoré has for the past ten years run his own commercial construction company in Baton Rouge, Louisiana, a trade he learned from his father. A leader with a deep sense of purpose, he devised some years ago a brilliant system to ensure that his values are reinforced in his company's culture. He figured out how to measure something most people can only pay lip service to:

work-life balance. Honoré believes that people should not spend all their time at work, but rather they should work to spend more of their time with their families.

Every employee at Honoré Construction is required to clock in in the morning and clock out in the evening. But there's a catch. They must clock in between 8:00–8:30 a.m. and out by 5:00–5:30 P.M. Stay any later and they are taken out of a bonus pool. Because employees know they have to leave by 5:30 p.m., wasted time has dropped to a minimum. Productivity is high and turnover is low. Consider how much you get done the day before you go on vacation. Now imagine every day is like that. That's what Dwayne Honoré figured out how to do. Because he figured out how to measure a value he holds dear, that value is embraced. Most importantly, because Honoré's actions pass the Celery Test, others can clearly see what he believes.

Money is a perfectly legitimate measurement of goods sold or services rendered. But it is no calculation of value. Just because somebody makes a lot of money does not mean that he necessarily provides a lot of value. Likewise, just because somebody makes a little money does not necessarily mean he provides only a little value. Simply by measuring the number of goods sold or the money brought in is no indication of value. Value is a feeling, not a calculation. It is perception. One could argue that a product with more bells and whistles that sells for less is the greater value. But by whose standard?

My uncle used to make tennis rackets. His rackets were made in the exact same factory as a name-brand racket. They were made of the same material on the same machine. The only difference was that when my uncle's rackets came off the assembly line, they didn't put the well-known brand logo on the product. My uncle's rackets sold for less money, in the same big-box retailer, next to the name-brand rackets. Month after month, the name-brand rackets outsold the generic-brand ones. Why? Because people perceived greater value from the name-brand rackets and felt just fine paying a premium for that feeling. On a strictly rational scale, the generic rackets offered better value. But again, value is a perception, not a calculation, which is the reason companies make such a big deal about investing in their brand. But a strong brand, like all other intangible factors that contribute to the perception of value, starts with a clear sense of WHY.

If those outside the megaphone share your WHY and if you are able to clearly communicate that belief in everything you say and do, trust emerges and value is perceived. When that happens, loyal buyers will always rationalize the premium they pay or the inconvenience they suffer to get that feeling. To them, the sacrifice of time or money is worth it. They will try to explain that their feeling of value comes from quality or features or some other easy-to-point-to element, but it doesn't. Those are external factors and the *feeling* they get comes completely from inside them. When people can point to a company and clearly articulate what the company believes and use words unrelated to price, quality, service and features, that is proof the company has successfully navigated the split. When people describe the value they perceive with visceral, excited words like "love," that is a sure sign that a clear sense of WHY exists.

Good Successions Keep the WHY Alive

There were three words missing from Bill Gates's goodbye speech when he officially left Microsoft in June 2008. They are three words he probably doesn't even realize need to be there.

"I'll be back."

Though Gates abdicated his role as CEO of Microsoft to Steve Ballmer in 2000 to lend more time and energy to the Bill and Melinda Gates Foundation, he still maintained a role and a presence at the Microsoft headquarters in Redmond, Washington. His plan was always to completely leave the company in the care of others, but like a lot of founders, Gates forgot to do one thing that would allow his plan to work. This one oversight could have a devastating impact on Microsoft and may even require him to come back someday to right the ship he built.

Bill Gates is special. Not just because of his brain or his management style. Though important, those two things alone are not the formula for building a $60 billion corporation from scratch. Like all visionary leaders, Bill Gates is special because he embodies what he believes. He is the personification of Microsoft's WHY. And for that reason, he serves as a physical beacon, a reminder of WHY everyone comes to work.

When Gates founded Microsoft with Paul Allen in 1975, he did so to advance a higher cause: if you give people the right tools, and make them more productive, then everyone, no matter their lot in life, will have an opportunity to achieve their real potential. "A PC in every home and on every desk," he envisioned; remarkable from a company that didn't even make PCs. He saw the PC as the great equalizer. Microsoft's most successful software, Windows, allowed anyone to have access to powerful technology. Tools like Word, Excel and PowerPoint gave everyone the power to realize the promise of the new technology—to become more efficient and productive. Small businesses, for example, could look and act like big businesses. Microsoft's software helped Gates advance his cause to empower the "everyman."

Make no mistake, Microsoft has done more to change the world than Apple. Though we are drawn to Apple's well-deserved reputation for innovation and challenging the business models of more than one industry, it is Microsoft that was responsible for the advancement of the personal computer. Gates put a PC on every desk and in doing so he changed the world. As the physical embodiment of the company's WHY, the "everyman" who fulfilled an amazing potential, what happens now that he's gone?

Gates himself has always held that he receives a "disproportionate" amount of attention for his role at Microsoft, much of it, of course, due to his exceptional wealth. Like all inspired leaders, he recognizes that his role is to lead the cause, but it is others who will be physically responsible for bringing that cause to life. Martin Luther King Jr. could not have changed America walking across a bridge in Selma, Alabama, with five prominent civil rights leaders. It took the thousands of people marching behind them to spur change. Gates recognizes the need for people to produce real change, but he neglected to remember that any effective movement, social or business, needs a leader to march in the front, preaching the vision and reminding people WHY they showed up in the first place. Though King needed to cross the bridge from Selma on his march to Montgomery, it was what it meant to cross the bridge that mattered. Likewise in business, though profit and shareholder value are valid and essential destinations, they do not inspire people to come to work.

Although Microsoft went through the split years ago, changing from a company that intended to change the world into a company that makes software, having Gates hanging around helped Microsoft maintain at least a loose sense of WHY they existed. With Gates gone, Microsoft does not have sufficient systems to measure and preach their WHY anymore. This is an issue that will have an exponential impact as time passes.

Such a departure as Gates's is not without precedent among companies with equally visionary leaders. Steve Jobs, the physical embodiment of the rabble-rousing revolutionary, a man who also personifies his company's WHY, left Apple in 1985 after a legendary power struggle with Apple's president, John Sculley, and the Apple board of directors. The impact on Apple was profound.

Originally hired by Jobs in 1983, Sculley was a perfectly capable executive with a proven track record. He knew WHAT to do and HOW to do things. He was considered one of the most talented marketing executives around, having risen quickly through the ranks of PepsiCo. At Pepsi, he created the wildly successful Pepsi Challenge taste test advertising campaign, leading Pepsi to overtake Coca-Cola for the first time. But the problem was, Sculley was a bad fit at Apple. He ran the company as a business and was not there to lead the cause.

It is worth considering how such a bad fit as Sculley even got the job at Apple in the first place. Simple—he was manipulated. Sculley did not approach Jobs and ask to be a part of Apple's cause. The way the real story unfolded made the fallout almost predictable. Jobs knew he needed help. He knew he needed a HOW guy to help him scale his vision. He approached Sculley, a man with a solid résumé, and said, "Do you want to sell sugar water your whole life or do you want to change the world?" Playing off Sculley's ego, aspirations and fears, Jobs completed a perfectly executed manipulation. And with it, Jobs was ousted from his own company a few years later.

Apple thrived on Steve Jobs's fumes for a few years as businesses started buying up Macintoshes and software developers continued to create new software. But it wouldn't be long until the company would begin to falter. Apple just wasn't what it used to be. It had gone through the split and ignored it. The WHY was getting fuzzier and fuzzier with each passing year. The inspiration was gone. Literally.

With a capable executive like Sculley running the business, there was no one to lead the cause. New products would be "less revolutionary and more evolutionary," reported *FORTUNE* magazine at the time, "some people might even call them dull." Weary of Apple's "right brain" ways, Sculley reorganized the company repeatedly, each time trying to get back what Apple clearly had lost. He brought in a new executive staff to help. But all they were doing was trying to manage HOW the company worked when it was the WHY that needed attention. Needless to say, morale was dismal. It wasn't until Jobs returned in 1997 that everyone inside and outside the company was reminded WHY Apple existed. With clarity back, the company quickly reestablished its power for innovation, for thinking different and, once again, for redefining industries. With Jobs at the helm again, the culture for challenging the status quo, for empowering the individual, returned. Every decision was filtered through the WHY, and it worked. Like most inspiring leaders, Jobs trusted his gut over outside advice. He was regularly criticized for not making mass-market decisions, such as letting people clone the Mac. He couldn't; those actions violated what he believed. They failed the Celery Test.

When the person who personifies the WHY departs without clearly articulating WHY the company was founded in the first place, they leave no clear cause for their successor to lead. The new CEO will come aboard to run the company and will focus attention on the growth of WHAT with little attention to WHY. Worse, they may try to implement their own vision without considering the cause that originally inspired most people to show up in the first place. In these cases, the leader can work against the culture of the company instead of leading or building upon it. The result is diminished morale, mass exodus, poor performance and a slow and steady transition to a culture of mistrust and every-man-for-himself.

It happened at Dell. Michael Dell, too, had a cause when he started his company. From the start, he focused on efficiency as a way of getting more computing power into more hands. Unfortunately, it was a cause that he too forgot, and then didn't communicate well enough before he stepped down as CEO of Dell Corp. in July 2004. After the company started to weaken—customer service, for one, plummeted—he came back in less than three years.

Michael Dell recognized that without him present to keep energy focused on the reason Dell Corp. was founded, the company became more obsessed with WHAT at the expense of WHY. "The company was too focused on the short term, and the balance of priorities was way too leaning toward things that deliver short-term results—that was the major root cause," Dell told the *New York Times* in September 2007. The company had in fact become so dysfunctional that some managers were compelled to falsify earnings reports between 2003 and 2006 in order to meet sales targets, suggesting a corporate culture that put undue pressure on managers to meet bottom-line targets. In the meantime, the company had missed significant market shifts, most notably the potential of the consumer market, and lost its edge with component suppliers as well. And in 2006, Hewlett-Packard swept past Dell as the largest seller of PCs worldwide. Dell had gone through the split and failed to recognize the reason it wasn't the company it used to be.

Starbucks is another good example. In 2000, Howard Schultz resigned as CEO of Starbucks, and for the first time in its history and despite 50 million customers per week, the company started to crack.

If you look back at the history of Starbucks, it thrived not because of its coffee but because of the experience it offered to customers. It was Schultz who brought that WHY to the company when he arrived in 1982, ten years after Gordon Bowker, Jerry Baldwin and Zev Siegl first started selling coffee beans in Seattle. In the early days it was about the coffee. Schultz, frustrated that the founders of Starbucks couldn't see the larger vision, set out to put the company on a new course, the course that ultimately turned Starbucks into the company we know today. Schultz had been enamored of the espresso bars of Italy, and it was his vision of building a comfortable environment between work and home, the "third space," as he called it, that allowed Starbucks to single-handedly create a coffee-shop culture in the United States that had until then only existed on college campuses.

That was the time when Starbucks stood for something. It reflected an underlying belief about the world. It was that idea that people bought, not the coffee. And it was inspiring. But Starbucks, like so many before it, went through the inevitable split. They, too, forgot about WHY the company was founded and started focusing on the results and the products. There was a time when Starbucks offered the option to sip your coffee out of a ceramic cup and eat your Danish off a ceramic plate. Two perfect details that helped bring the company's belief to life in the place between work and home. But ceramic crockery is expensive to maintain and Starbucks did away with it, favoring the more efficient paper cups. Though it saved money, it came at a cost: the erosion of trust. Nothing says to a customer "We love you, now get out" like a paper cup. It was no longer about the third space. It had become about the coffee. The company's WHY was going fuzzy. Thankfully, Schultz was there, the physical embodiment of the WHY, to remind people of the higher cause. But in 2000 he left, and things got worse.

Starbucks had grown from fewer than 1,000 stores to 13,000 in only ten years. Eight years and two CEOs later, the company was dangerously overextended just as it was facing an onslaught of competition from McDonald's, Dunkin' Donuts and other unexpected places. In a now famous memo that Schultz wrote to his successor, Jim Donald, just months before returning to take the helm, he implored Donald to "make the changes necessary to evoke the heritage, the tradition and the passion that we all have for the true Starbucks experience." The reason the company was floundering was not that it grew too fast, but that Schultz had not properly infused his WHY into the organization so that the organization could manage the WHY without him. In early 2008, Schultz replaced Donald with a leader who could better steer the company back to a time before the split: himself.

None of these executives are considered God's gift to management. Steve Jobs's paranoia, for example, was well documented, and Bill Gates is socially awkward. Their companies are thousands of people deep and they alone can't pull all the strings or push all the buttons to make everything work properly. They rely on the brains and the management skills of teams of people to help them build their megaphones. They rely on people who share their cause. In this respect, they are no different from other executives. But what they all have in common, something that not all CEOs possess, is that they physically embody the cause around which they built their companies. Their physical presence reminds every executive and every employee WHY they show up to work. Put simply: they inspire. Yet, like Bill Gates, these inspired leaders have all failed to properly articulate their cause in words that others could rally around in their absence. Failing to put the movement into hard words leaves them as the only ones who can lead the movement. What happens when Dell or Schultz leave again? What will happen now that Jobs has passed?

For companies of any size, success is the greatest challenge. As Microsoft grew, Gates stopped talking about what he believed and how he was going to change the world and started talking about what the company was doing. Microsoft changed. Founded as a company that believed in making people more productive so they could achieve their highest potential, Microsoft became a company that simply made software products. Such a seemingly subtle change affects behaviors. It alters decisions. And it impacts how a company structures itself for the future. Though Microsoft had changed since its founding, the impact was never as dramatic because at least Bill Gates was there, the physical embodiment of the cause that inspired his executives and employees.

Microsoft is just one of the tangible things Gates has done in his life to bring his cause to life. The company is one of the WHATs to his WHY. And now he's off to do something else that also embodies his cause—to use the Gates Foundation to help people around the world wake up every day to overcome obstacles so they too can have an opportunity to achieve their potential. The only difference is he's not doing it with software anymore. Steve Ballmer, a smart man by all accounts, does not physically embody Gates's vision of the world. He has the image of a powerful executive who sees numbers, competitors and markets. He is a man with a gift for managing the WHAT line. Like John Sculley at Apple, Jim Donald at Starbucks and Kevin Rollins at Dell—all the CEOs who replaced the visionary founders or executives—Ballmer might be the perfect man to work alongside a visionary, but is he the perfect man to replace one?

The entire culture of all these companies was built around one man's vision. The only succession plan that will work is to find a CEO who believes in and wants to continue to lead that movement, not replace it with their own vision of the future. Ballmer knows how to rally the company, but can he inspire it?

Successful succession is more than selecting someone with an appropriate skill set—it's about finding someone who is in lockstep with the original cause around which the company was founded. Great second or third CEOs don't take the helm to implement their own vision of the future; they pick up the original banner and lead the company into the next generation. That's why we call it succession, not replacement. There is a continuity of vision.

One of the reasons Southwest Airlines has been so good at succession is because its cause is so ingrained in its culture, and the CEOs who took over from Herb Kelleher also embodied the cause. Howard Putnam was the first president of Southwest after Kelleher. Though he was a career airline guy, it was not his résumé that made him so well suited to lead the company. He was a good fit. Putnam recounts the time he met with Kelleher to interview for the job. Putnam leaned back in his chair and noticed that Kelleher had slipped his shoes off under the desk. More significantly, Putnam noticed the hole in one of Kelleher's socks. It was at that point that Putnam felt he was the right man for the job. He loved that Kelleher was just like everyone else. He too had holes in his socks.

Although Putnam felt Southwest was right for him, how do we know if he was right for Southwest? I had a chance to spend half a day with Putnam to talk. At one point in the afternoon I suggested we take a break and grab a Starbucks. The mere suggestion incensed him. "I'm not going to Starbucks!" he cracked. "I'm not paying five dollars for a cup of coffee. And what the heck is a Frappuccino anyway?" It was at that point I realized how perfect a fit Putnam was for Southwest. He was an everyman. A Dunkin' Donuts guy. He was a perfect man to take the torch from Kelleher and charge forward. Southwest inspired him. In the case of Howard Putnam, Kelleher hired somebody who could represent the cause, not reinvent it.

Today it has become so acculturated there that it's almost automatic. The same could be said for Colleen Barrett, who became president of Southwest in 2001, some thirty years after she was working as Kelleher's secretary in his San Antonio law firm. By 2001, the company had nearly 30,000 employees and a fleet of 344 planes. By the time she took over, Barrett says that running the company had become "a very collective effort." Kelleher stopped his day-to-day involvement in the company, but left a corporate culture so strong that his presence in the hallways was no longer needed. The physical person had largely been replaced by the folklore of Kelleher. But it is the folklore that has helped keep the WHY alive. Barrett freely admits she's not the smartest executive out there. She is self-deprecating in her personal assessment, in fact. But as the leader of the company, being the smartest was not her job. Her job was to lead the cause. To personify the values and remind everyone WHY they are there.

The good news is, it will be easy to know if a successor is carrying the right torch. Simply apply the Celery Test and see if what the company is saying and doing makes sense. Test whether WHAT they are doing effectively proves WHY they were founded. If we can't easily assess a company's WHY simply from looking at their products, services, marketing and public statements, then odds are high that they don't know what it is either. If they did, so would we.

When the WHY Goes, WHAT Is All You'll Have Left

On April 5, 1992, at approximately eight in the morning, Wal-Mart lost its WHY. On that day, Sam Walton, Wal-Mart's inspired leader, the man who embodied the cause around which he built the world's largest retailer, died in the University of Arkansas Medical Science Hospital in Little Rock of bone marrow cancer. Soon after, Walton's oldest son, S. Robeson Walton, who succeeded his father as chairman of the company, gave a public statement. "No changes are expected in the corporate direction, control or policy," he said. Sadly for Wal-Mart employees, customers and shareholders, that is not what happened.

Sam Walton was the embodiment of the everyman. Though he was named the richest man in America by *Forbes* magazine in 1985, a title he held until he died, he never understood the importance others placed on money. Certainly, Walton was a competitor, and money was a good yardstick of success. But that's not what gave Walton or those who worked at Wal-Mart the feeling of success. It was people Walton valued above all else. People.

Look after people and people will look after you was his belief, and everything Walton and Wal-Mart did proved it. In the early days, for example, Walton insisted on showing up for work on Saturdays out of fairness to his store employees who had to work weekends. He remembered birthdays and anniversaries and even that a cashier's mother had just undergone gallbladder surgery. He chastised his executives for driving expensive cars and resisted using a corporate jet for many years. If the average American didn't have those things, then neither should those who are supposed to be their champions.

Wal-Mart never went through a split under Walton's command, because Walton never forgot where he came from. "I still can't believe it was news that I get my hair cut at the barbershop. Where else would I get it cut?" he said. "Why do I drive a pickup truck? What am I supposed to haul my dogs around in, a Rolls-Royce?" Often seen wearing his signature tweed jacket and a trucker's cap, Walton was the embodiment of those he aimed to serve—the average-Joe American.

With a company so beloved by employees, customers and communities, Walton made only one major blunder. He didn't put his cause into clear enough words so that others could continue to lead the cause after he died. It's not entirely his fault. The part of the brain that controls the WHY doesn't control language. So, like so many, the best Walton could articulate was HOW to bring his cause to life. He talked about making products cheap to make things more affordable to the average working American. He talked about building stores in rural communities so that the backbone of America's workforce didn't have to travel to the urban centers. It all made sense. All his decisions passed the Celery Test. It was the WHY upon which the company was built, however, that was left unsaid.

Walton was involved in the company until just before his death, when his ailing health prevented him from participating any longer. Like all organizations with founder-leaders whose physical presence helps keep the WHY alive, his continued involvement in the company had reminded everyone WHY they came to work every day. He inspired everyone around him. Just as Apple ran on the fumes of Steve Jobs for a few years after he left the company before significant cracks started to show, so did Wal-Mart remember Sam Walton and his WHY for a short time after he died. But as the WHY started to get fuzzier and fuzzier, the company changed direction. From then on, there would be a new motivation at the company, and it was something that Walton himself cautioned against: chasing money.

Costco was cofounded in 1983 by WHY-type Jim Sinegal and HOW-type Jeffrey Brotman. Sinegal learned about discount retailing from Sol Price, the same person from whom Sam Walton admitted to "borrowing" much of what he knew about the business. And, like Walton, Sinegal believes in people first. "We're going to be a company that's on a first-name basis with everyone," he said in an interview on ABC's newsmagazine show *20/20*. Following the same formula as other inspiring leaders, Costco believes in looking after its employees first. Historically, they have paid their people about 40 percent more than those who work at Sam's Club, the Wal-Mart–owned discount warehouse. And Costco offers above-average benefits, including health coverage for more than 90 percent of their employees. As a result, their turnover is consistently five times lower than Sam's Club.

Like all companies built around a cause, Costco has relied on their megaphone to help them grow. They don't have a PR department and they don't spend money on advertising. The Law of Diffusion is all that Costco needed to get the word out. "Imagine that you have 120,000 loyal ambassadors out there who are constantly saying good things about you," quips Sinegal, recognizing the value of trust and loyalty of his employees over advertising and PR.

For years, Wall Street analysts criticized Costco's strategy of spending so much on their people instead of on cutting costs to boost margins and help share value. Wall Street would have preferred the company to focus on WHAT they did at the expense of WHY they did it. A Deutsche Bank analyst told *FORTUNE* magazine, "Costco continues to be a company that is better at serving the club member and employee than the shareholder."

Fortunately, Sinegal trusts his gut more than he trusts Wall Street analysts. "Wall Street is in the business of making money between now and next Tuesday," he said in the *20/20* interview. "We're in the business of building an organization, an institution that we hope will be here fifty years from now. And paying good wages and keeping people working with you is very good business."

The amazing insight in all of this is not just how inspiring Sinegal is, but that almost everything he says and does echoes Sam Walton. Wal-Mart got as big as it did doing the exact same thing—focusing on WHY and ensuring that WHAT they did proved it. Money is never a cause, it is always a result. But on that fateful day in April 1992, Wal-Mart stopped believing in their WHY.

Since Sam Walton's death, Wal-Mart has been battered by scandals of mistreating employees and customers all in the name of shareholder value. Their WHY has gone so fuzzy that even when they do things well, few are willing to give them credit. The company, for example, was among the first major corporations to develop an environmental policy aimed at reducing waste and encouraging recycling. But Wal-Mart's critics have grown so skeptical of the company's motives that the move was largely dismissed as posturing. "Wal-Mart has been working to improve its image and lighten its environmental impact for several years now," a column published on the *New York Times* Web site on October 28, 2008, read. "Wal-Mart is still selling consumerism even as it pledges to cut the social and environmental costs of making the stuff in its stores." Costco, on the other hand, was later than Wal-Mart to announce an environmental policy, yet has received a disproportionate amount of attention. The difference is that people *believe* it when Costco does it. When people know WHY you do WHAT you do, they are willing to give you credit for everything that could serve as proof of WHY. When they are unclear about your WHY, WHAT you do has no context. Even though the things you do or decisions you make may be good, they won't make sense to others without a clear understanding of WHY.

And what of the results? Still running on the memory of Sam Walton, Wal-Mart's culture stayed intact at first, and the value of the two stocks was about even for a few years after Walton died. But as Wal-Mart continued to run its business in a post-Sam, post-split manner while Costco maintained clarity of WHY, the difference in value changed dramatically. An investment in Wal-Mart on the day Sam Walton died would have earned a shareholder a 300 percent gain by the time this book was written. An investment made in Costco on the same day would have netted an 800 percent gain.

Costco's advantage is that the embodiment of their WHY, Jim Sinegal, is still there. The things he says and does help reinforce to all those around him what the company stands for. Staying true to that WHY, Sinegal draws a $430,000 salary, a relatively small amount given the size and success of the company. At Wal-Mart's peak, Sam Walton never took a salary of more than $350,000 per year, also consistent with what he believed. David Glass, the first man to take over as CEO after Sam Walton, a man who had spent considerable time around Walton, said, "A lot of what goes on these days with high-flying companies and these overpaid CEOs, who're really just looting from the top and aren't watching out for anybody but themselves, really upsets me. It's one of the main things wrong with American business today."

Three more CEOs have attempted to carry the torch that Walton lit. And with each succession that torch, that clear sense of purpose, cause and belief, has grown dimmer and dimmer. The new hope lies in Michael T. Duke, who took over as CEO in early 2009. Duke's goal is to restore the luster and the clarity of Wal-Mart's WHY.

And to do it, he started by paying himself an annual salary of $5.43 million.

PART 6

DISCOVER WHY

13

THE ORIGINS OF A WHY

It started in Vietnam War–era Northern California, where antigovernment ideals and disdain for large centers of power ran rampant. Two young men saw the power of government and corporations as the enemy, not because they were big, per se, but because they squashed the spirit of the individual. They imagined a world in which an individual had a voice. They imagined a time when an individual could successfully stand up to incumbent power, old assumptions and status quo thoughts and successfully challenge them. Even redirect them. They hung out with hippie types who shared their beliefs, but they saw a different way to change the world that didn't require protesting or engaging in anything illegal.

Steve Wozniak and Steve Jobs came of age in this time. Not only was the revolutionary spirit running high in Northern California, but it was also the time and place of the computer revolution. And in this technology they saw the opportunity to start their own revolution. "The Apple gave an individual the power to do the same things as any company," Wozniak recounts. "For the first time ever, one person could take on a corporation simply because they had the ability to use the technology." Wozniak engineered the Apple I and later the Apple II to be simple enough for people to harness the power of the technology. Jobs knew how to sell it. Thus was born

Apple Computer. A company with a purpose—to give the individual to power to stand up to established power. To empower the dreamers and the idealists to challenge the status quo and succeed. But their cause, their WHY, started long before Apple was born.

In 1971, working out of Wozniak's dorm room at UC Berkeley, the two Steves made something they called the Blue Box. Their little device hacked the phone system to give people the ability to avoid paying long-distance rates on their phone bills. Apple computers didn't exist yet, but Jobs and Woz were already challenging a Big Brother–type power, in this case Ma Bell, American Telephone and Telegraph, the monopoly phone company. Technically, what the Blue Box did was illegal, and with no desire to challenge power by breaking the law, Jobs and Woz never actually used the device themselves. But they liked the idea of giving other individuals the ability to avoid having to play by the rules of monopolistic forces, a theme that would repeat many more times in Apple's future.

On April 1, 1976, they repeated their pattern again. They took on the giants of the computer industry, most notably Big Blue, IBM. Before the Apple, computing still meant using a punch card to give instructions to a huge mainframe squirreled away in a computer center somewhere. IBM targeted their technology to corporations and not, as Apple intended, as a tool for individuals to target corporations. With clarity of purpose and amazing discipline, Apple Computer's success seemed to follow the Law of Diffusion almost by design. In its first year in business, the company sold $1 million worth of computers to those who believed what they believed. By year two, they had sold $10 million worth. By their third year in business they were a $100 million company, and they attained billion-dollar status within only six years.

Already a household name, in 1984 Apple launched the Macintosh with their famed "1984" commercial that aired during the Super Bowl. Directed by Ridley Scott, famed director of cult classics like *Blade Runner*, the commercial also changed the course of the advertising industry. The first "Super Bowl commercial," it ushered in the annual tradition of big-budget, cinematic Super Bowl advertising. With the Macintosh, Apple once again changed the tradition of how things were done. They challenged the standard of Microsoft's DOS, the standard operating system used by most personal computers at the time. The Macintosh was the first mass-market computer to use a graphical user interface and a mouse, allowing people to simply "point and click" rather than input code. Ironically, it was Microsoft that took Apple's concept to the masses with Windows, Gates's version of the graphical user interface. Apple's ability to ignite revolutions and Microsoft's ability to take ideas to the mass market perfectly illustrate the WHY of each company and indeed their respective founders. Jobs had always been about challenge and Gates has always been about getting to the most people.

Apple would continue to challenge with other products that followed the same pattern. Recent examples include the iPod and, more significantly, iTunes. With these technologies, Apple challenged the status quo business model of the music industry—an industry so distracted trying to protect its intellectual property and their outdated business model that it was busy suing thirteen-year-old music pirates while Apple redefined the online music market. The pattern repeated again when Apple introduced the iPhone. The status quo dictated that the cellular providers and not the phone manufacturer decide the features and capabilities of the actual phones. T-Mobile, Verizon Wireless, and Sprint, for example, tell Motorola, LG, and Nokia what to do. Apple changed all that when they announced that, with the iPhone, they would be telling the provider what the phone would do. Ironically the company that Apple challenged with their Blue Box decades before, this time around exhibited classic early-adopter behavior. AT&T was the only one to agree to this new model, and so another revolution was ignited.

Apple's keen aptitude for innovation is born out of its WHY and, save for the years Jobs was missing (1985 and 1997), it has never changed since the company was founded. Industries holding on to legacy business models should be forewarned; you could be next. If Apple stays true to their WHY, the television and movie industries will likely be next.

Apple's ability to do what they do has nothing to do with industry expertise. All computer and technology companies have open access to talent and resources and are just as qualified to produce all the products Apple does. It has to do with a purpose, cause or belief that started many years ago with a couple of idealists in Cupertino, California. "I want to put a ding in the universe," as Steve Jobs put it. And that's exactly what Apple did in the industries in which it competes. Apple was born out of its founders' WHY. There is no difference between one or the other. Apple was just one of the WHATs to Jobs's and Woz's WHY. The personalities of Jobs and Apple are exactly the same. In fact, the personalities of all those who are viscerally drawn to Apple are similar. There is no difference between an Apple customer and an Apple employee. One believes in Apple's WHY and chooses to work for the company, and the other believes in Apple's WHY and chooses to buy its products. It is just a behavioral difference. Loyal shareholders are no different either. WHAT they buy is different, but the reason they buy and remain loyal is the same. The products of the company become symbols of their own identities. The die hards outside the company are said to be a part of the cult of Apple. The die hards inside the company are said to be a part of some sort of cult. Their symbols are different, but their devotion to the cause is the same. That we use the word "cult" implies that we can recognize that there is a deep faith, something irrational, that all those who believe share. And we'd be right. Jobs, his company, his loyal employees and his loyal customers all exist to push the boundaries. They all fancy a good revolution. And even though Jobs is no longer at the helm, his cause cannot die if Apple is to continue to stand out.

Just because Apple's WHY is so clear does not mean everyone is drawn to it. Some people like them and some don't. Some people embrace them and some are repelled by them. But it cannot be denied: they stand for something. The Law of Diffusion says that only 2.5 percent of the population has an innovator mentality— they are a group of people willing to trust their intuition and take greater risks than others. Perhaps it is no coincidence that Microsoft Windows sits on 96 percent of the world's computers whereas Apple maintains about 2.5 percent. Most people don't want to challenge the status quo.

Though Apple employees will tell you the company's success lies in its products, the fact is that a lot of companies make quality products. And though Apple's employees may still insist that their products are better, it depends on the standard by which you are judging them. Apple's products are indeed best for those who relate to Apple's WHY. It is Apple's belief that comes through in all they think, say and do that makes them who they are. They are so effective at it, they are able to clearly identify their own products simply by preceding the product name with the letter "i." But they don't just own the letter, they own the *word* "I." They are a company that champions the creative spirit of the individual, and their products, services and marketing simply prove it.

The WHY Comes from Looking Back

Conservative estimates put the numbers at three to one. But some historians have said the English army was outnumbered by six to one. Regardless of which estimates you choose to believe, the prospects for Henry V, king of England, did not look good. It was late October in the year 1415 and the English army stood ready to do battle against a much bigger French force at Agincourt in northern France. But the numbers were just one of Henry's problems.

The English army had marched over 250 miles, taking them nearly three weeks, and had lost nearly 40 percent of their original numbers to sickness. The French, in stark contrast, were better rested and in much better spirits. The better-trained and more experienced French were also excited at the prospect of exacting their revenge on the English to make up for the humiliation of previous defeats. And to top it all off, the French were vastly better equipped. The English were lightly armored, but whatever protection they did have was no match for the superior weight of the French armor. But anyone who knows their medieval European history already knows the outcome of the battle of Agincourt. Despite the overwhelming odds, the English won.

The English had one vital piece of technology that was able to confound the French and start a chain of events that would ultimately result in a French defeat. The English had the longbow, a weapon with astounding range for its time. Standing far from the battlefield, far enough away that heavy armor was not needed, the English could look down into the valley and shower the French with arrows. But technology and range aren't what give an arrow its power. By itself, an arrow is a flimsy stick of wood with a sharpened tip and some feathers. By itself, an arrow cannot stand up to a sword or penetrate armor. What gives an arrow the ability to take on experience, training, numbers and armor is momentum. That flimsy stick of wood, when hurtling through the air, becomes a force only when it is moving fast in one direction. But what does the battle of Agincourt have to do with finding your WHY?

Before it can gain any power or achieve any impact, an arrow must be pulled backward, 180 degrees away from the target. And that's also where a WHY derives its power. The WHY does not come from looking ahead at what you want to achieve and figuring out an appropriate strategy to get there. It is not born out of any market research. It does not come from extensive interviews with customers or even employees. It comes from looking in the completely opposite direction from where you are now. Finding WHY is a process of discovery, not invention.

Just as Apple's WHY developed during the rebellious 1960s and '70s, the WHY for every other individual or organization comes from the past. It is born out of the upbringing and life experience of an individual or small group. Every single person has a WHY and every single organization has one too. An organization, don't forget, is one of the WHATs, one of the tangible things a founder or group of founders has done in their lives to prove their WHY.

Every company, organization or group with the ability to inspire starts with a person or small group of people who were inspired to do something bigger than themselves. Gaining clarity of WHY, ironically, is not the hard part. It is the discipline to trust one's gut, to stay true to one's purpose, cause or beliefs. Remaining completely in balance and authentic is the most difficult part. The few that are able to build a megaphone, and not just a company, around their cause are the ones who earn the ability to inspire. In doing so, they harness a power to move people that few can even imagine. Learning the WHY of a company or an organization or understanding the WHY of any social movement always starts with one thing: you.

I Am a Failure

There are a few months indelibly printed in my memory—September to December 2005. This was when I hit rock bottom.

I started my business in February 2002 and it was incredibly exciting. I was "full of piss and vinegar," as my grandfather would say. From an early age, my goal was to start my own business. It was the American Dream, and I was living it. My whole feeling of self-worth came from the fact that I did it, I took the plunge, and it felt amazing. If anyone ever asked me what I did, I would pose like George Reeves from the old *Superman* TV series. I would put my hands on my hips, stick out my chest, stand at an angle and with my head raised high I'd declare, "I am an entrepreneur." What I did was how I defined myself, and it felt good. I wasn't like Superman, I was Superman.

As anyone who starts a business knows, it is a fantastic race. There is a statistic that hangs over your head—over 90 percent of all new businesses fail in the first three years. For anyone with even a bit of a competitive spirit in them, especially for someone who defines himself or herself as an entrepreneur (hands on hips, chest out, standing at a slight angle), these overwhelming odds of failure are not intimidating, they only add fuel to the fire. The foolishness of thinking that you're a part of the small minority of those who actually will make it past three years and defy the odds is part of what makes entrepreneurs who they are, driven by passion and completely irrational.

After year one, we celebrated. We hadn't gone out of business. We were beating the odds. We were living the dream. Two years passed. Then three years. I'm still not sure how we did it—we never properly implemented any good systems and processes. But to heck with it, we'd beaten the odds. I had achieved my goal and that's all that mattered. I was now a proud member of a very small group of people who could say, with statistical proof, that I was an American small business owner.

The fourth year would prove to be very different. The novelty of being an entrepreneur had worn off. I no longer stood like George Reeves. When asked what I did, I would now tell people that I did "positioning and strategy consulting." It was much less exciting and it certainly didn't feel like a big race anymore. It was no longer a passionate pursuit, it was just a business. And the reality was that the business did not look that rosy.

We were never a runaway success. We made a living, but not much more. We had some FORTUNE 500 clients and we did good work. I was crystal clear on what we did. And I could tell you how we were different—how we did it. Like everyone else in the game, I would try to convince prospective clients how we did it, how we were better, how our way was unique . . . and it was hard work. The truth is, we beat the odds because of my energy, not because of my business acumen, but I didn't have the energy to sustain that strategy for the rest of my life. I was aware enough to know that we needed better systems and processes if the business was to sustain itself.

I was incredibly demoralized. Intellectually, I could tell you what I needed to do, I just couldn't do it. By September 2005 I was the closest I've ever been to, if I wasn't already, completely depressed. My whole life I'd been a pretty happy-go-lucky guy, so just being unhappy was bad enough. But this was worse.

The depression made me paranoid. I was convinced I was going to go out of business. I was convinced I was going to be evicted from my apartment. I was certain anyone who worked for me didn't like me and that my clients knew I was a fraud. I thought everyone I met was smarter than me. I thought everyone I met was better than me. Any energy I had left to sustain the business now went into propping myself up and pretending that I was doing well.

If things were to change, I knew I needed to learn to implement more structure before everything crashed. I attended conferences, read books and asked successful friends for advice on how to do it. It was all good advice, but I couldn't hear it. No matter what I was told, all I could hear was that I was doing everything wrong. Trying to fix the problem didn't make me feel better, it made me feel worse. I felt more helpless. I started having desperate thoughts, thoughts that for an entrepreneur are almost worse than suicide: I thought about getting a job. Anything. Anything that would stop the feeling of falling I had almost every day.

I remember visiting the family of my future brother-in-law for Thanksgiving that year. I sat on the couch in the living room of his mother's house, people were talking to me, but I never heard a word. If I was asked questions, I replied only in platitudes. I didn't really desire or even have the ability to make conversation anymore. It was then that I realized the truth. Statistics notwithstanding, I was a failure.

As an anthropology major in college and a strategy guy in the marketing and advertising world, I had always been curious about why people do the things they do. Earlier in my career I started becoming curious about these same themes in the real world—in my case, corporate marketing. There is an old saying in the industry that 50 percent of all marketing works, the problem is, which 50 percent? I was always astounded that so many companies would operate with such a level of uncertainty. Why would anyone want to leave the success of something that costs so much, with so much at stake to the flip of a coin? I was convinced that if some marketing worked, it was possible to figure out why.

All companies of equal resources have equal access to the same agencies, the same talent, and the same media, so why does some marketing work and some doesn't? Working in an ad agency I'd seen it all the time. With conditions relatively equal, the same team could develop a campaign that would be hugely successful one year, then develop something the next year that would do nothing. Instead of focusing on the stuff that didn't work, I chose to focus on the stuff that worked to find out what it all had in common. The good news for me was there was not much to study.

How has Apple been able to so consistently outmarket their competition over and over and over? What did Harley-Davidson do so well that they were able to create a following of people so loyal that they would tattoo a corporate logo on their bodies? Why did people love Southwest Airlines so much—they aren't really *that* special . . . are they? In an attempt to codify why these worked, I developed a simple concept I called the Golden Circle. But my little theory sat buried in my computer files. It was a little pet project with no real application, just something I found interesting.

It would be months later that I met a woman at an event who took an interest in my perspectives in marketing. Victoria Duffy Hopper grew up in an academic family and also has a lifelong fascination with human behavior. She was the first to tell me about the limbic brain and the neocortex. My curiosity piqued by what she was telling me, I started reading about the biology of the brain, and it was then that I made the real discovery.

The biology of human behavior and the Golden Circle overlapped perfectly. While I was trying to understand why some marketing worked and some didn't, I had tripped over something vastly more profound. I discovered why people do what they do.

It was then that I realized what was the real cause of my stress. The problem wasn't that I didn't know what to do or how to do it, the problem was I had forgotten WHY. I had gone through what I now know is a split, and I needed to rediscover my WHY.

To Inspire People to Do the Things That Inspire Them

Henry Ford said, "If you think you can or you think you can't, you're right." He was a brilliant WHY-guy who changed the way industry works. A man who embodied all the characteristics of a great leader, who understood the importance of perspective. I wasn't any dumber than I was when I started my business, probably the opposite, in fact. What I had lost was perspective. I knew what I was doing, but I had forgotten WHY. There is a difference between running with all your heart with your eyes closed and running with your all your heart with your eyes wide open. For three years, my heart had pounded but my eyes had been closed. I had passion and energy, but I lacked focus and direction. I needed to remember what inspired my passion.

I became obsessed with the concept of WHY. I was consumed by the idea of it. It was all I talked about. When I looked back to my upbringing, I discovered a remarkable theme. Whether among friends, at school or professionally, I was always the eternal optimist. I was the one who inspired everyone to believe they could do whatever they wanted. This pattern is my WHY. To inspire. It didn't matter if I was doing it in marketing or consulting. It didn't matter what types of companies I worked with or in which industries I worked. To inspire people to do the things that inspired them, so that, together, we can change the world. That's the path to which my life and my work is now completely devoted. Henry Ford would have been proud of me. After months of thinking I couldn't, now I knew I could.

I made myself a guinea pig for the concept. If the reason I hit rock bottom was because my Golden Circle was out of balance, then I needed to get it back in balance. If it was important to start with WHY, then I would start with WHY in everything I did. There is not a single concept in this book that I don't practice. I stand at the mouth of my megaphone and I talk about the WHY to anyone who will listen. Those early adopters who hear my cause see me as a tool in their arsenal to achieve their own WHY. And they introduced me to others whom they believed I could inspire. And so the Law of Diffusion started to do its job.

Though the Golden Circle and the concept of WHY was working for me, I wanted to show it to others. I had a decision to make: do I try to patent it, protect it and use it to make lots of money, or do I give it away? This decision was to be my first Celery Test. My WHY is to inspire people to do the things that inspire them, and if I am to be authentic to that cause there was only one decision to make—to give it away, to talk about it, to share it. There would never be any secret sauce or special formula for which only I knew the ingredients. The vision is to have every person and every organization know their WHY and use it to benefit all they do. So that's what I'm doing, and I'm relying entirely on the concept of WHY and the naturally occurring pattern that is the Golden Circle to help me get there.

The experiment started to work. Prior to starting with WHY, I had been invited to give one public speech in my life. Now I get between thirty and forty invitations per year, from all sorts of audiences, all over the world, to speak about the Golden Circle. I speak to audiences of entrepreneurs, large corporations, nonprofits, in politics and government. I've spoken at the Pentagon to the chief of staff and the secretary of the Air Force. Prior to the Golden Circle, I didn't even know anyone in the military. Prior to starting with WHY, I had never been on television; in fewer than two years I started getting regular invitations to appear on MSNBC. I've worked with members of Congress, having never done any government or political work prior to starting with WHY.

I am the same person. I know the same things I did before. The only difference is, now I start with WHY. Like Gordon Bethune who turned around Continental with the same people and the same equipment, I was able to turn things around with the things I already knew and did.

I'm not better connected than everyone else. I don't have a better work ethic. I don't have an Ivy League education and my grades in college were average. The funniest part is, I still don't know how to build a business. The only thing that I do that most people don't is I learned how to start with WHY.

14

THE NEW COMPETITION

If You Follow Your WHY, Then Others Will Follow You

"BANG!" The gun fires and the race is on. The runners take off across the field. It rained the day before and the ground is still damp. The temperature is cool. It is a perfect day for running. The line of runners quickly forms a pack. Like a school of fish they come together as one. They move as one. The pack sets a pace to maximize their energy for the whole race. As with any race, in a short period of time the stronger ones will start to pull ahead and the weaker ones will start to fall behind. But not Ben Comen. Ben was left behind as soon as the starter gun sounded. Ben's not the fastest runner on the team. In fact, he's the slowest. He has never won a single race the entire time he's been on the Hanna High School cross-country track team. Ben, you see, has cerebral palsy.

Cerebral palsy, a condition often caused by complications at birth, affects someone's movement and balance. The physical problems endure for a lifetime. Misshapen spines create a twisted posture. Muscles are often withered and motor reflexes slow. Tightness in the muscles and joints also affect balance. Those with cerebral palsy often have an unsteady gait, their knees knock and their feet drag. To an outsider, they may seem clumsy. Or even broken.

The pack pulls farther and farther ahead while Ben falls farther and farther behind. He slips on the wet grass and falls forward into the soft earth. He slowly picks himself up and keeps going. Down he goes again. This time it hurts. He gets back up and keeps running. Ben won't quit. The pack is now out of sight and Ben is running alone. It is quiet. He can hear his own labored breathing. He feels lonely. He trips over his own feet again, and down he goes yet another time. No matter his mental strength, there is no hiding the pain and frustration on his face. He grimaces as he uses all his energy to pull himself back to his feet to continue running. For Ben, this is part of the routine. Everyone else finishes the race in about twenty-five minutes. It usually takes Ben more than forty-five minutes.

When Ben eventually crosses the finish line he is in pain and he is exhausted. It took every ounce of strength he had to make it. His body is bruised and bloodied. He is covered in mud. Ben inspires us, indeed. But this is not a story of "when the going gets tough, the tough get going." This is not a story of "when you fall down, pick yourself up." Those are great lessons to learn, without a doubt, but we don't need Ben Comen to teach us those lessons. There are dozens of others we can look to for that, like an Olympic athlete, for example, who suffered an injury just months before the games only to come back to win a medal. Ben's lesson is deeper.

Something amazing happens after about twenty-five minutes. When everybody else is done with their race, everyone comes back to run with Ben. Ben is the only runner who, when he falls, someone else will help pick him up. Ben is the only runner who, when he finishes, has a hundred people running behind him.

What Ben teaches us is special. When you compete against everyone else, no one wants to help you. But when you compete against yourself, everyone wants to help you. Olympic athletes don't help each other. They're competitors. Ben starts every race with a very clear sense of WHY he's running. He's not there to beat anyone but himself. Ben never loses sight of that. His sense of WHY he's running gives him the strength to keep going. To keep pushing. To keep getting up. To keep going. And to do it again and again and again. And every day he runs, the only time Ben sets out to beat is his own.

Now think about how we do business. We're always competing against someone else. We're always trying to be better than someone else. Better quality. More features. Better service. We're always comparing ourselves to others. And no one wants to help us. What if we showed up to work every day simply to be better than ourselves? What if the goal was to do better work this week than we did the week before? To make this month better than last month? For no other reason than because we want to leave the organization in a better state than we found it?

All organizations start with WHY, but only the great ones keep their WHY clear year after year. Those who forget WHY they were founded show up to the race every day to outdo someone else instead of to outdo themselves. The pursuit, for those who lose sight of WHY they are running the race, is for the medal or to beat someone else.

What if the next time when someone asks, "Who's your competition?" we replied, "No idea." What if the next time someone pushes, "Well, what makes you better than your competition?" we replied, "We're not better than them in all cases." And what if the next time someone asks, "Well, why should I do business with you then?" we answer with confidence, "Because the work we're doing now is better than the work we were doing six months ago. And the work we'll be doing six months from now will be better than the work we're doing today. Because we wake up every day with a sense of WHY we come to work. We come to work to inspire people to do the things that inspire them. Are we better than our competition? If you believe what we believe and you believe that the things we do can help you, then we're better. If you don't believe what we believe and you don't believe the things we can do will help you, then we're not better. Our goal is to find customers who believe what we believe and work together so that we can all succeed. We're looking for people to stand shoulder-to-shoulder with us in pursuit of the same goal. We're not interested in sitting across a table from each other in pursuit of a sweeter deal. And here are the things we're doing to advance our cause . . ." And then the details of HOW and WHAT you do follow. But this time, it started with WHY.

Imagine if every organization started with WHY. Decisions would be simpler. Loyalties would be greater. Trust would be a common currency. If our leaders were diligent about starting with WHY, optimism would reign and innovation would thrive. As this book illustrates, there is precedence for this standard. No matter the size of the organization, no matter the industry, no matter the product or the service, if we all take some responsibility to start with WHY and inspire others to do the same, then, together, we can change the world.

And that's pretty inspiring.

· · ·

If this book inspired you, please pass it on to someone you want to inspire.

BE A PART OF THIS MOVEMENT, SHARE YOUR VISION OF THE WORLD

Before any person or organization can take the steps necessary to be a leader, we must first agree on a definition of what a leader is. Leadership is not about power or authority. Leadership is decidedly more human. Being a leader requires one thing and one thing only: followers. A follower is someone who volunteers to go where you are going. They choose to go not because they have to, not because they were incentivized to, not because they were threatened to, but because they want to. The question is, why would anyone follow you?

If an individual or organization hopes to assume the responsibility of leadership—a responsibility that is given, not taken—then they must think, act, and speak in a way that inspires people to follow. Leadership is always about people. No one leads a company. A company is a legal structure. You can run a company, you can manage an organization, but you can lead only people. And that requires two things.

Imagine we're out on a boat tour with a group of strangers and the boat gets stranded on a deserted island. How will we get off the island? Some people are panicking, some people are starting to form little cliques to figure out how to get off the island. Then, all of a sudden one person stands up and announces, "I will lead." We like that; we're social animals and we respond well to leaders.

Our new leader moves to the front of the group and asks, "Right . . . who's got ideas?"

One person raises her hand and suggests we light a fire to attract the attention of a passing boat or aircraft. "Good idea," our leader says.

Another person pipes up, "We should forage for food in case we're stuck here for a while."

"Also a good idea," says the leader.

"We should build a shelter because we're going to need protection from the elements."

Our leader gives a thumbs-up and says, "That's also a good idea. OK," he continues, "let's take a vote. . . ."

And at that point someone in the group stands up and says, "As we were coming into shore, I saw some masts and smoke out on the west side of the island. There must be a fishing village there. If we can get there, we can get help. We're going to have to go through the thick woods to get there, though, and I can't do it alone. So if there is anyone who will join me, I'd be grateful. If anyone doesn't want to go," he says, "don't worry, we'll come back to get you when we find help."

The question is, whom do you want to follow? Do you want to follow the first guy or the second guy? Both are confident. Both care that we get off the island. The answer is so obvious it's almost a silly question: we want to follow the second guy.

Keep in mind, no one else saw the fishing village. There are no photographs and no research. All we have is the undying belief of this one person of a world that exists in the future and his ability to communicate it in a way that lets us imagine it as clearly.

All leaders must have two things: they must have a vision of the world that does not exist and they must have the ability to communicate it. The second leader could have simply stood up, with the same vision of this fishing village, and simply announced, "This won't work," and walked away in the direction of the village. He would have been a visionary, for sure, but without the ability to communicate his vision, he cannot be a leader. We all work with people like this—they walk around with all the answers to all the questions, frustrated that no one else "gets it." No one can see what they can see. They are visionaries, for sure, but they are not leaders.

There are also those who have the gift of gab, the amazing ability to communicate. But absent a vision, they are just great communicators and not leaders. The second leader could have also stood up and given a rousing speech about the importance of us working together. We would have felt wonderful and excited, but we would still have no clue how to get off the island.

Leadership requires two things: a vision of the world that does not yet exist and the ability to communicate it.

The question is, where does vision come from? And this is the power of WHY. Our visions are the world we imagine, the tangible results of what the world would look like if we spent every day in pursuit of our WHY.

Leaders don't have all the great ideas; they provide support for those who want to contribute. Leaders achieve very little by themselves; they inspire people to come together for the good of the group. Leaders never start with what needs to be done. Leaders start with WHY we need to do things. Leaders inspire action.

ACKNOWLEDGMENTS

There is nothing that brings me more joy and happiness in this world than waking up every day with a clear sense of WHY—to inspire people to do the things that inspire them. It is a simple thing to do when surrounded by so many amazing people to inspire me.

There are countless people who believed in me and helped me over the years. I'd like to thank those who helped me build a piece of my megaphone with this book. Amy Hertz was the first to insist that I write it and introduced me to my incredible agent, Richard Pine. Richard believes in doing good things in the world and has made it his business to make authors out of those who have a positive message to share. His patience and counsel have been invaluable. To Russ Edelman who was such a nice guy to introduce me to his editor, Jeffrey Krames, who, in turn, took a bet on me and let me push him to do things differently. To Adrian Zackheim, who willingly challenges convention and is leading the evolution of the publishing industry.

Thank you to Mark Rubin, who sees the colors I can see and in whose basement I started writing, to Tom and Alicia Rypma, in whose home I continued writing, and to Delta Air Lines, for being so good to me while I wrote so much at 35,000 feet. To Julia Hurley, who made sure everything was right. To the whole team at Portfolio, who worked so hard to bring this book to life. And, most importantly, to Laurie Flynn, who so passionately devoted herself (and her family) to help me tell this story.

I have had the great honor and privilege of meeting some wonderful people who have inspired me in a way that is hard to quantify. Ron Bruder has changed the way I see the world. Brig. Gen. Lori Robinson has shown me what the humility of great leadership looks like. Kim Harrison, who lives her WHY—to appreciate all good things around her—and works tirelessly to see to it that good ideas and people are appreciated. She taught me what a true partnership looks and feels like. And to those whose shared what they know to help bring the WHY to life, I am truly grateful for your time and energy: Colleen Barrett, Gordon Bethune, Ben Comen, Randy Fowler, Christina Harbridge, Dwayne Honoré, Howard Jeruchimowitz, Guy Kawasaki, Howard Putnam, Acacia Salatti, Jeff Sumpter, James Tobin, Col. "Cruiser" Wilsbach and Steve Wozniak.

Long before there was even an idea of a book, there were all the people and early adopters who wanted to learn about the WHY and use the Golden Circle to help build their organizations. This forward-thinking group were willing to embrace a new idea and were essential to helping me figure out many of the details and nuances of the concept. Thank you to Geoffrey Dzikowski, Jenn Podmore, Paul Guy, Kal Shah, Victor DeOliveria, Ben Rosner, Christopher Bates, Victor Chan, Ken Tabachnick, Richard Baltimore, Rick Zimmerman, Russ Natoce, Missy Shorey, Morris Stemp, Gabe Solomon, Eddie Esses and Elizabeth Hare, who saw the value of the WHY in building the most valuable organization of all—her family. Thank you to Fran Biderman-Gross, who is not only an early adopter, but who went out of her way to embrace her WHY in all aspects of her life and to encourage others to learn their WHY, too. Thank you to Congresswoman Stephanie Herseth Sandlin, Congressman Paul Hodes, and Congresswoman Allyson Schwartz, who gave me so much and continue to give back to others with such passion.

Over the years there were those who gave me a break and helped advance my cause. Thank you to Trudi Baldwin, the director of the Graduate Program in Strategic Communications at Columbia University (a wonderful program); Jim Berrien, who trusted me; the indefatigable Jack Daly, who teaches me; Piers Fawkes; Denis Glennon, who pushed me; Kevin Goetz; Tony Gomes; Paul Gumbinner, who gave me a career on a silver platter; Kenneth Hein; Peter Intermaggio, who taught me self-reliance; Pamela Moffat; Rick Sapio, who keeps doing good things for me; Alana Winter and Matt Weiss, for asking me to share my thoughts with an audience; and Diederik Werdmolder who took a bet on me right at the start.

I am grateful to all the brilliant minds I have met within the U.S. Air Force who stuck their necks out to try something different. They embody the WHY of the USAF: to find and deliver better ways of doing things. To Maj. Gen. Erwin Lessel (who first introduced me to the organization), Maj. Gen. William Chambers, Brig. Gen. Walter Givhan, Brig. Gen. Dash Jamieson (who never stops believing), Maj. Gen. Darren McDew, Brig. Gen. (Sel) Martin Neubauer (who knows more than I will ever know), Christy Nolta, Brig. Gen. Janet Therianos and Lt. Col. DeDe Halfhill (you owe me one, DeDe).

I am immensely grateful to all the brilliant people and candid conversations that inspired so many of the ideas that became the Golden Circle and all its parts. Thank you to Kendra Coppey, who helped me out of the hole in late 2005 and to Mark Levy, who pointed me in the right direction. Thanks to Peter Whybrow, who saw a problem in America and helped me to understand the neuroscience of it all. Kirt Gunn, whose brilliant storytelling mind inspired the split. Every conversation with Brian Collins illuminated something new. Thank you to Jorelle Laakso, who taught me to reach for the things I believe in. To William Ury, who showed me a path to follow, and Lt. Gen. David Deptula, who is probably the smartest person I know and gave me a new perspective for solving highly complex problems.

My understanding of the WHY would be incomplete without the conversations, help and support of Nic Askew, Richard Baltimore, Christopher Bennett, Christine Betts, Ariane de Bonvoisin, Scott Bornstein, Tony Conza, Vimal Duggal, Douglas Feirstein, Nathan Frankel, JiNan Glasgow, Cameron Herold, John Hittler, Maurice Kaspy, Kevin Langley, Peter Laughter, Niki Lemon, Seth Lloyd, Bruce Lowe, Cory Luker, Karl and Agi Mallory, Peter Martins, Brad Meltzer, Nell Merlino, Ally Miller, Jeff Morgan, Alan Remer, Pamela and Nick Roditi, Ellen Rohr, Lance Platt, Jeff Rothstein, Brian Scudamore, Andy Siegel, John Stepleton, Rudy Vidal, the 2007 and 2008 classes of the Gathering of Titans, and the one and only Ball of Mystery.

To my late grandfather, Imre Klaber, who showed me that it is more fun to be slightly eccentric than to be completely normal. To my parents, Steve and Susan Sinek, who always encouraged me to follow the beat of my own drum. And to Sara, my remarkable, remarkable sister, who appreciates that I keep my head in the clouds but makes sure I keep my feet on the ground.

There are a few books and authors that have, over the years, inspired me, spurred ideas and offered me new perspectives: the works of Ken Blanchard, of Tom Friedman and of Seth Godin, *The Starfish and the Spider* by Ori Brafman and Rod Beckstrom, *First, Break All the Rules* by Marcus Buckingham, *Good to Great* by Jim Collins, *The 7 Habits of Highly Effective People* by Stephen Covey, *The 4-Hour Workweek* by Tim Ferriss, *Never Eat Alone* by Keith Ferrazzi, *E-Myth* by Michael Gerber, *The Tipping Point* and *Outliers* by Malcolm Gladwell, *Chaos* by James Gleick, *Emotional Intelligence* by Daniel Goleman, *Made to Stick* by Chip and Dan Heath, *Who Moved My Cheese?* by Spencer Johnson, M.D., *The Monk and the Riddle* by Randy Komisar, *The Five Dysfunctions of a Team* by Patrick Lencioni, *Freakonomics* by Steven D. Levitt and Stephen J. Dubner, *FISH!* By Stephen Lundin, Harry Paul, John Christensen and Ken Blanchard, *The Naked Brain* by Richard Restack, *Authentic Happiness* by Martin Seligman, *The Wisdom of*

Crowds by James Surowiecki, *The Black Swan* by Nicholas Taleb, *American Mania* by Peter Whybrow, M.D., and the single most important book everyone should read, the book that teaches us that we cannot control the circumstances around us, all we can control is our attitude—*Man's Search for Meaning* by Viktor Frankl.

I want to especially thank all those people who have joined this cause and actively work to inspire those around you. I am grateful for all the e-mails and notes you send me. I save them all as a reminder that it takes lots and lots of people, standing shoulder to shoulder, to have a real impact.

And finally, to all those who read this book and pass it on to someone you believe it will inspire, thank you. I know that if enough of us learn about the existence of the WHY and work hard to start everything we do with WHY, we can and will change the world.

NOTES

Chapter 1: Assume You Know

14   *In the United States, a line worker would take a rubber mallet and tap the edges of the door*: Norman Bodek, "What is Muda?" *Manufacturing Engineering*, July 2006, http://www.sme.org/cgi-bin/find-articles.pl?&ME06ART40&ME&2006 0709&SME.

Chapter 2: Carrots and Sticks

19   *By 2007, Toyota's share had climbed to 16.3 percent*: Tom Krisher, "GM, Toyota in virtual tie on 2007 sales," *USA Today*, January 23, 2008, http://www.usatoday .com/money/topstories/2008-01-23-434472425_x.htm.

19   *In 2007, GM lost $729 per vehicle*: Oliver Wyman's Harbour Report 2008, http:// www.oliverwyman.com/content_images/OW_EN_Automotive_Press_2008_ HarbourReport08.pdf.

20   *nearly 40 percent of those customers never get the lower price*: Brian Grow, "The Great Rebate Runaround," *BusinessWeek*, November 23, 2005, http://www .businessweek.com/bwdaily/dnflash/nov2005/nf20051123_4158_db016.htm.

22   *"Quitting smoking is the easiest thing I've ever done"*: American Cancer Society Guide to Quitting Smoking, http://www.cancer.org/docroot/PED/content/ PED_10_13X_Guide_for_Quitting_Smoking.asp.

24   *a Tag Heuer watch designed "especially for the golfer"*: http://www.tagheuer.com/ the-collection/specialists/golf-watch/index.lbl.

24   *Nike's "I wanna be like Mike" campaign*: "The Allure of Gatorade," *CNN Money*, November 22, 2000, http://money.cnn.com/2000/11/21/deals/gatorade/.

25   *"In a major innovation in design and engineering"*: "Introducing the Motorola RAZR V3," http://www.motorola.com/mediacenter/news/detail.jsp?globalObj ectId=4485_3818_23.

26   *Less than four years later, Zander was forced out*: "Motorola's Zander out after 4 rocky years," MSNBC, November 30, 2007, http://www.msnbc.msn.com/ id/22040026/.

27   *Colgate offers a link on their Web site*: http://www.colgate.com/app/Colgate/US/ OC/Products/Toothpastes/Name.cvsp.

29   *Samsung, the electronics giant*: "Samsung's American Unit Settles Rebate Case,"

New York Times, October 21, 2004, http://query.nytimes.com/gst/fullpage
.html?res=9B01E3DD113AF932A15753C1A9629C8B63.

33 *Rather, Whybrow says, it's the way that corporate America has developed*: Peter C.
Whybrow, *American Mania: When More Is Not Enough.* New York: W. W. Norton & Company, 2005.

Chapter 3: The Golden Circle

37 *the golden ratio—a simple mathematical relationship*: Wolfram Mathworld,
"Golden Ratio," http://mathworld.wolfram.com/GoldenRatio.html. Also
http://goldennumber.net/.

38 *John F. Kennedy's challenge to put a man on the moon*: "The Decision to Go the
Moon: President John F. Kennedy's May 25, 1961 Speech before a Joint Session
of Congress," NASA History Office, http://history.nasa.gov/moondec.html.

44 *"1,000 songs in your pocket"*: "Apple Presents iPod," http://www.apple.com/pr/
library/2001/oct/23ipod.html.

44 *The multigigabyte portable hard drive music player was actually invented by Creative Technology Ltd.*: "The Nomad Jukebox Holds a Hefty Store of Music," *New
York Times,* June 1, 2000, http://www.nytimes.com/2000/06/01/technology/
news-watch-the-nomad-jukebox-holds-a-hefty-store-of-music.html?scp=
1&sq=creative+nomad&st=nyt.

46 *Apple even changed its legal name in 2007*: "Apple Debuts iPhone, TV Device,
Drops 'Computer' From Name," Foxnews.com, January 11, 2007, http://www
.foxnews.com/story/0,2933,242483,00.html.

Chapter 4: This Is Not Opinion, This Is Biology

52 *Now, the Star-Belly Sneetches*: Dr. Seuss, *The Sneetches and Other Stories.* New
York: Random House, 1961.

54 *U2 and Apple belong together*: "Apple Introduces the U2 iPod," http://www
.apple.com/pr/library/2004/oct/26u2ipod.html.

54 *"I'm a Mac and I'm a PC"*: "Get a Mac," http://www.apple.com/getamac/ads/.

57 *Richard Restak, a well-known neuroscientist*: Richard Restak, MD, *The Naked
Brain: How the Emerging Neurosociety Is Changing How We Live, Work and
Love.* New York: Harmony, 2006.

Chapter 5: Clarity, Discipline and Consistency

70 *to take what Pacific Southwest was doing in California*: "PSA: Catch Our Smile;
The Story of Pacific Southwest Airlines," http://catchoursmile.com/.

70 *In nearly every way, King and Kelleher were opposites*: Matt Malone, "In for a
Landing," Portfolio.com, August 2008, http://www.portfolio.com/executives/
features/2008/07/16/Q-and-A-with-Southwest CEO-Kelleher; Joseph Guinto,
"Rollin On," *Southwest Airlines Spirit,* June 2006, http://macy.ba.ttu.edu/
Fall%2006/SWA%20Rollin%20On.pdf; Katrina Brooker, "The Chairman of the
Board Looks Back," *FORTUNE,* May 28, 2001, http://money.cnn.com/maga
zines/fortune/fortune_archive/2001/05/28/303852/index.htm; "We Weren't Just
Airborne Yesterday," http://www.southwest.com/about_swa/airborne.html.

71 *In the early 1970s, only 15 percent of the traveling population traveled by air*:
Brian Lusk, Southwest Airlines manager of customer communications, personal correspondence, February 2009.

72   *Howard Putnam, one of the former presidents of Southwest*: Howard Putnam, personal interview, October 2008.

Chapter 6: The Emergence of Trust

83   *Throughout the 1980s, this was life at Continental Airlines*: Gordon Bethune, *From Worst to First: Behind the Scenes of Continental's Remarkable Comeback.* New York: John Wiley and Sons, 1999.

83   *Happy employees ensure happy customers*: Kevin Freiberg and Jackie Freiberg, *Nuts! Southwest Airlines' Crazy Recipe for Business and Personal Success.* New York: Broadway, 1998.

85   *"You don't lie to your own doctor"*: Gordon Bethune, personal interview, January 2009.

91   *The cost . . . would be about $250,000*: "Shackleton Plans Record Polar Trip," *New York Times*, December 30, 1913.

91   *Donations from English schoolchildren paid for the dog teams*: "Ernest H. Shackleton, 1874–1922," South-Pole.com, www.south-pole.com/p0000097.htm.

91   *Just a few days out of South Georgia Island*: http://www.pbs.org/wgbh/nova/shackleton/1914/timeline.html.

91   *"like an almond in a piece of toffee"*: Paul Ward, "Shackleton, Sir Ernest (1874–1922)," Cool Antarctica, http://www.coolantarctica.com/Antarctica%20fact%20file/History/Ernest%20Shackleton_Trans-Antarctic_expedition2.htm.

92   *"Men wanted for Hazardous journey"*: Nova Online, http://www.pbs.org/wgbh/nova/shackleton/1914/team.html.

94   *In the 1970s, Southwest Airlines decided to put their flight attendants in hot pants*: Howard Putnam, personal interview, October 2008.

96   *Langley assembled some of the best and brightest minds of the day*: James Tobin, *To Conquer the Air: The Wright Brothers and the Great Race for Flight.* New York: Free Press, 2004.

97   *Langley saw the airplane as his ticket to fame and fortune*: Tobin, personal interview, February 2009.

97   *"Wilbur and Orville were true scientists"*: Tobin, personal interview, February 2009.

98   *He found the defeat humiliating*: Tobin, *To Conquer the Air.*

101   *Southwest Airlines is famous for pioneering the ten-minute turnaround*: Paul Burnham Finney, "Loading an Airliner is Rocket Science," *New York Times*, November 14, 2006, http://travel2.nytimes.com/2006/11/14/business/14boarding.html?pagewanted=print.

103   *"People at the London end of Barings"*: Nick Leeson and Edward Whitley. *Rogue Trader: How I Brought Down Barings Bank and Shook the Financial World.* New York: Little, Brown and Company, 1996.

105   *Southwest will not tolerate customers who abuse their staff*: Freiberg and Freiberg, *Nuts!*

106   *A one-star general, John Jumper was an experienced F-15 pilot*: General Lori Robinson, personal interview, October 2008.

108   *he served as chief of staff of the U.S. Air Force from 2001 to 2005*: http://www.af.mil/bios/bio.asp?bioID=5986.

108   *Now herself a brigadier general in the Air Force*: http://www.af.mil/bios/bio.asp?bioID=10439.

Chapter 7: How a Tipping Point Tips

115 *In 2000, Malcolm Gladwell created his own tipping point*: Malcolm Gladwell, *The Tipping Point: How Little Things Can Make a Big Difference.* New York: Back Bay Books, 2002.

116 *Everett M. Rogers was the first to formally describe how innovations spread through society*: Everett M. Rogers, *Diffusion of Innovations.* New York: Free Press, 2003.

116 *Geoffrey Moore expanded on Rogers's ideas to apply the principle to high-tech product marketing*: Geoffrey A. Moore, *Crossing the Chasm.* New York: Collins, 2002.

122 *In 1997, TiVo was racing to market with a remarkable new device*: John Markoff, "Netscape Pioneer to Invest in Smart VCR," *New York Times,* November 9, 1998, http://query.nytimes.com/gst/fullpage.html?res=9F0DE0D6133EF93AA35752 C1A96E958260.

123 *TiVo finally shipped in 1999*: http://www.tivo.com/abouttivo/aboutushome/ index.html.

123 *TiVo sold about 48,000 units the first year*: Roy Furchgott, "Don't People Want to Control Their TV's?" *New York Times,* August 24, 2000, http://www.nytimes .com/2000/08/24/technology/don-t-people-want-to-control-their-tv-s.html.

123 *"More U.S. Homes Have Outhouses than TiVos"*: Bradley Johnson, "Analysts Mull Future Potential of PVR Ad-Zapping Technology," *Advertising Age,* November 4, 2002, http://people.ischool.berkeley.edu/~hal/Courses/StratTech09/ Lectures/Networks/Articles/tivo-losing-money.html.

128 *"There are two types of laws"*: Martin Luther King Jr., "Letter from a Birmingham Jail," http://www.thekingcenter.org/prog/non/Letter.pdf.

Chapter 8: Start with Why, but Know How

133 *Steve Ballmer, the man who replaced Bill Gates as CEO of Microsoft*: "Steve Ballmer Going Crazy," March 31, 2006, http://www.youtube.com/watch?v=wvs boPUjrGc.

134 *the Bill and Melinda Gates Foundation*: http://www.gatesfoundation.org/Pages/ home.aspx.

135 *Raised in Ohio, sixty miles from Dayton, Neil Armstrong grew up*: Nick Greene, "Neil Armstrong Biography: First Man of the Moon," About.com, http://space .about.com/od/astronautbiographies/a/neilarmstrong.htm.

138 *What Ralph Abernathy lent the movement was something else*: "Abernathy, Ralph David (1926–1990)," Martin Luther King, Jr., Research and Education Institute, http://mlk-kpp01.stanford.edu/index.php/kingpapers/article/abernathy_ ralph_david_1926_1990/.

140 *The pessimists are usually right*: Thomas Friedman, *The World Is Flat: A Brief History of the 21st Century.* New York: Farrar, Straus and Giroux, 2005.

140 *"If it hadn't been for my big brother"*: Bob Thomas, *Building a Company: Roy O. Disney and the Creation of an Entertainment Empire.* New York: Disney Editions, 1998.

142 *Herb Kelleher was able to personify and preach the cause of freedom*: Kevin Freiberg and Jackie Freiberg, *Nuts! Southwest Airlines' Crazy Recipe for Business and Personal Success.* New York: Broadway, 1998.

142 *Steve Wozniak is the engineer who made the Apple work*: Steve Wozniak, personal interview, November 2008.

143 *Bill Gates and Paul Allen went to high school together in Seattle*: Randy Alfred,

"April 4, 1975: Bill Gates, Paul Allen Form a Little Partnership," *Wired*, April 4, 1975, http://www.wired.com/science/discoveries/news/2008/04/dayintech_0404.

145   *Oprah Winfrey once gave away a free car*: Ann Oldenburg, "7M car giveaway stuns TV audience," *USA Today*, September 13, 2004, http://www.usatoday .com/life/people/2004-09-13-oprah-cars_x.htm.

150   *the Education for Employment Foundation*: http://www.efefoundation.org/ homepage.html; Lisa Takeuchi Cullen, "Gainful Employment," *Time*, September 20, 2007, http://www.time.com/time/magazine/article/0,9171,1663851,00 .html; Ron Bruder, personal interview, February 2009.

Chapter 10: Communication Is Not About Speaking, It's About Listening

160   *"I Have a Dream" speech*: "I Have a Dream—Address at March on Washington, August 28, 1963. Washington, D.C.," MLK Online, http://www.mlkonline.net/ dream.html.

160   *American flag on a soldier's right arm?*: Brendan I. Koerner, "Soldiers and Their Backward Flags," *Slate*, March 18, 2003, http://www.slate.com/id/2080338/.

161   *"Don't let anyone tell you that America's best days are behind her"*: President Ronald Reagan's Address Before a Joint Session of the Congress Reporting on the State of the Union, January 26, 1982, http://www.c-span.org/executive/ transcript.asp?cat=current_event&code=bush_admin&year=1982.

163   *"Mostly, it says I'm an American"*: Randy Fowler, general manager of a Harley-Davidson dealership in California, personal interview, January 2009.

165   *In 2003 and 2004 Apple ran a promotion for iTunes with Pepsi*: http://www .apple208m/pr/library/2003/oct/16pepsi.html.

170   *Volkswagen introduced a $70,000 luxury model to their lineup*: "2006 Volkswagen Phaeton Review," Edmonds.com., http://www.edmunds.com/volkswagen/ phaeton/2006/review.html; "VW analyses Phaeton failure, reveals new details about next-gen model," MotorAuthority.com, February 18, 2008, http://www .motorauthority.com/vw-analyses-phaeton-failure-reveals-new-details-about-next-gen-model.html.

Chapter 11: When Why Goes Fuzzy

175   *"A lot of what goes on these days with high-flying companies"*: Sam Walton and John Huey, *Sam Walton: Made in America; My Story.* New York: Bantam, 1992.

176   *There are 27.7 million registered businesses in the United States today*: U.S. Small Business Administration, Office of Advocacy, http://www.sba.gov/advo/stats/ sbfaq.pdf.

176   *Sam Walton didn't even invent a better way of doing things than everyone else*: Bob Ortega, *In Sam We Trust: The Untold Story of Sam Walton and How Wal-Mart Is Devouring the World.* New York: Kogan Page, 1999.

177   *For Sam Walton, there was something else*: Walton and Huey, *Sam Walton.*

177   *"We're all working together; that's the secret"*: http://walmartstores.com/ CommunityGiving/8508.aspx.

177   *The company once renowned for how it treated employees and customers has been scandal-ridden for nearly a decade*: "Wal-Mart Wage and Hour Settlement," *Wal-Mart Watch*, http://action.walmartwatch.com/page/-/Wal-Mart%20Wage%20 and%20Hour%20Settlement.pdf.

178   *"Celebrate your successes"*: Gene N. Landrum, *Entrepreneurial Genius: The Power of Passion*. New York: Brendan Kelly Publishing Inc., 2004.

178   *Wal-Mart still sells more than six times as much as Target each year*: http://walmartstores.com/FactsNews/NewsRoom/8224.aspx; http://investors.target.com/phoenix.zhtml?c=65828&p=irol-homeProfile.

179   *Every year a group of high-performing entrepreneurs get together at MIT's Endicott House*: http://www.gatheringoftitans.com/.

Chapter 12: Split Happens

189   *In the fall of her freshman year in college, Christina Harbridge set out to find a part-time job*: Christina Harbridge, personal interview, November 2008; http://christinaharbridge.com/blog/.

191   *Dwayne Honoré has for the past ten years run his own commercial construction company*: Dwayne Honoré, personal interview, December 2008; http://www.dhonore.com/explore.cfm/ourcompany/owner/.

193   *Though Gates abdicated his role as CEO*: "Gates exits Microsoft to focus on charity work," MSNBC News Services, June 27, 2008, http://www.msnbc.msn.com/id/25408326/.

194   *"A PC in every home and on every desk"*: http://www.microsoft.com/about/companyinformation/ourbusinesses/profile.mspx.

195   *after a legendary power struggle with Apple's president, John Sculley*: Andrew Pollack, "Apple Computer Entrepreneur's Rise and Fall," *New York Times*, September 19, 1985, http://query.nytimes.com/gst/fullpage.html?res=950DE7DA1739F93AA2575AC0A963948260&scp=3&sq=apple%201985%20jobs%20resigns&st=cse.

195   *Sculley was a perfectly capable executive with a proven track record*: "Marketing Genius for Pepsi and Apple: John Sculley III, WG'63," *Wharton Alumni Magazine*, Spring 2007, http://www.wharton.upenn.edu/alum_mag/issues/125anniversaryissue/sculley.html.

196   *"Do you want to sell sugar water your whole life or do you want to change the world?"*: *Triumph of the Nerds*: The Television Program Transcripts: Part III, PBS, http://www.pbs.org/nerds/part3.html.

196   *New products would be "less revolutionary and more evolutionary"*: Brian O'Reilly, "Apple Computer's Risky Revolution," *FORTUNE*, May 8, 1989, http://money.cnn.com/magazines/fortune/fortune_archive/1989/05/08/71954/index.htm.

197   *From the start, he focused on efficiency*: Steve Lohr, "Can Michael Dell Refocus His Namesake?" *New York Times*, September 9, 2007, http://www.nytimes.com/2007/09/09/technology/09dell.html.

198   *If you look back at the history of Starbucks*: http://www.starbucks.com/aboutus/Company_Timeline.pdf.

199   *In a now famous memo that Schultz wrote*: "Text of Starbucks Memo," *Wall Street Journal*, February 24, 2007, http://online.wsj.com/public/article/SB117234084129218452-hpbDoP_cLbOUdcG_0y7qLlQ7Okg_20080224.html?mod=rss_free.

199   *In early 2008, Schultz replaced Donald*: Burt Helm and Jena McGregor, "Howard Schultz's Grande Challenge," *BusinessWeek*, January 9, 2008, http://www.businessweek.com/magazine/content/08_03/b4067000369003.htm?chan=top+news_top+news+index_businessweek+exclusives.

201   *Putnam recounts the time he met with Kelleher to interview for the job*: Howard Putnam, personal interview, October 2008.

201   *The same could be said for Colleen Barrett, who became president of Southwest in 2001*: Colleen Barrett, personal interview, December 2008.

202   *Walton's oldest son, S. Robeson Walton*: http://findarticles.com/p/articles/mi_m3092/is_n8_v31/ai_12098902/.

203   *Walton insisted on showing up for work on Saturdays*: Sam Walton and John Huey, *Sam Walton: Made in America; My Story*. New York: Bantam, 1992.

203   *"I still can't believe it was news that I get my hair cut at the barbershop"*: Ibid.

204   *Sinegal learned about discount retailing from Sol Price*: Matthew Boyle, "Why Costco is so addictive," *FORTUNE*, October 25, 2006, http://money.cnn.com/magazines/fortune/fortune_archive/2006/10/30/8391725/index.htm.

204   *Sinegal believes in people first*: Alan B. Goldberg and Bill Ritter, "Costco CEO Finds Pro-Worker Means Profitability," ABC News, August 2, 2006, http://abcnews.go.com/2020/business/story?id=1362779.

204   *Wall Street analysts criticized Costco's strategy of spending so much on their people*: John Helyar, "The Only Company Wal-Mart Fears," *FORTUNE*, November 24, 2003, http://money.cnn.com/magazines/fortune/fortune_archive/2003/11/24/353755/index.htm.

205   *"Wal-Mart has been working to improve its image and lighten its environmental impact for several years now"*: Andrew C. Revkin, "Wal-Mart's New Sustainability Push," nytimes.com, October 23, 2008, http://dotearth.blogs.nytimes.com/tag/wal-mart/.

206   *"A lot of what goes on these days with high-flying companies"*: Walton and Huey, *Sam Walton*.

206   *And to do it, he started by paying himself an annual salary of $5.43 million*: http://finance.yahoo.com/q/pr?s=WMT.

Chapter 13: The Origins of a WHY

209   *"The Apple gave an individual the power to do the same things as any company"*: Steve Wozniak, personal interview, November 2008.

210   *the two Steves made something they called the Blue Box*: Nick Cantlay, "Biography: Stephen Wozniak," The Apple Museum, http://www.theapplemuseum.com/index.php?id=50.

210   *famed "1984" commercial that aired during the Super Bowl*: http://www.youtube.com/watch?v=OYecfV3ubP8.

Chapter 14: The New Competition

222   *But not Ben Comen*: Rick Reilly, "Worth the Wait," *Sports Illustrated*, http://sportsillustrated.cnn.com/2003/pr/subs/siexclusive/rick_reilly/10/13/reilly1020/index.html _the_wait.htm.

INDEX